ENGLISH SPOKEN HERE

Life in the United States

Jerry L. Messec
Roger E. Kranich

CAMBRIDGE Adult Education
Prentice Hall Regents, Englewood Cliffs, NJ 07632

Executive Editor: Brian Schenk
Project Editors/Writers: Eva Holzer
Cynthia Ward
Project Consultants: Laurel T. Ellis
Don Williams
Art Direction: Taurins Design Associates
Artists: Kathryn Yingling (two-page spreads)
Linda Miyamoto
Miki McCarron

© 1982 by Prentice Hall Regents
Published by Prentice-Hall, Inc.
A Division of Simon & Schuster
Englewood Cliffs, New Jersey 07632

Printed in the United States of America

10 9 8 7 6 5 4 3 2

Prentice-Hall International (UK) Limited, *London*
Prentice-Hall of Australia Pty. Limited, *Sydney*
Prentice-Hall Canada Inc., *Toronto*
Prentice-Hall Hispanoamericana, S.A., *Mexico*
Prentice-Hall of India Private Limited, *New Delhi*
Prentice-Hall of Japan, Inc., *Tokyo*
Simon & Schuster Asia Pte. Ltd., *Singapore*
Editora Prentice-Hall do Brasil, Ltda., *Rio de Janeiro*

ISBN: 0-8428-0853-1

CONTENTS

UNIT 1

WHO'S IN CHARGE?

IN THIS UNIT, YOU WILL BE:

opening and using bank accounts

mailing letters and packages

talking about rules

disagreeing with and expressing anger
toward someone

trying to calm someone down

asking for and giving advice

talking about what is possible, probable,
and impossible

In the Close-Up on Language, you will
review:

the verb forms you use to talk about and
ask about things that happen in the
present (present, present continuous,
present perfect, and present perfect
continuous)

LOOK AT THE PICTURE.
Find these things in the picture.

1. teller
2. teller's window
3. bank officer
4. loan application form
5. safety deposit boxes
6. vault
7. deposit and withdrawal slips
8. checkbook
9. closed-circuit camera
10. wastebasket

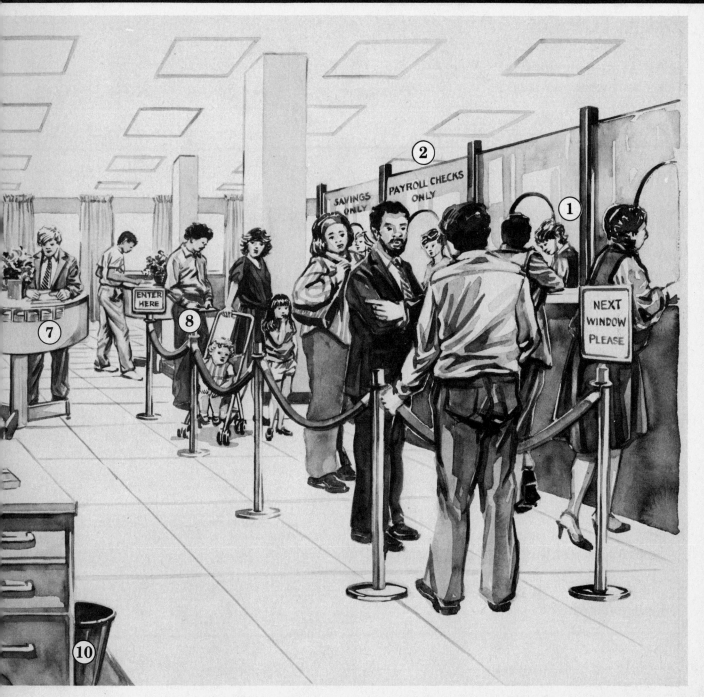

1

TALK TOPICS

LOOK AT THE PICTURE.
Talk about what you see.

What is this place?
Why are the customers standing in line?
Where are the tellers?   Where are the bank
    officers?

Talk about your experiences in a bank.
What kinds of accounts do you have?
Have you ever applied for a bank loan?
Do you have a safety deposit box?
What kinds of special banking services do
    you use?

Do you think that it's safe to keep money in
    a bank?   Why?
Would you recommend putting money in a
    savings account?
When would you pay interest to the bank?
    When would the bank pay you interest?

How are banks in the United States different
    from the banks in your native country?

Pretend to be one of the people in the
    picture.   What were you doing in the
    picture on page 1?   What are you doing
    in this picture?   If you are talking, what
    are you saying?

ASK QUESTIONS ABOUT THE PICTURE.
Write down the new words and expressions you want to remember.

11. _____
12. _____
13. _____
14. _____
15. _____

16. _____
17. _____
18. _____
19. _____
20. _____

OPENING A BANK ACCOUNT

LISTEN TO THESE PEOPLE.
They are talking about opening bank accounts.

CARLA: I'd like to open a checking account.

BANK OFFICER: Fine. I'll need some information for our application form. What is your name, please?

CARLA: Carla Dimona. D-I-M-O-N-A.

BANK OFFICER: What's your address, Ms. Dimona?

CARLA: 481 Holly Lane, Lafayette, 70502.

BANK OFFICER: And your Social Security number?

CARLA: It's 131-84-6730.

BANK OFFICER: Are you a U.S. citizen? Where and when were you born?

CARLA: I'm an Italian citizen. I was born in Naples on July 23, 1960.

BANK OFFICER: May I have the name and address of your employer?

CARLA: I work for Capitol Industries, 500 Main Avenue, Lafayette, 70502.

BANK OFFICER: I also need your home phone number and your work number, Ms. Dimona.

CARLA: My home phone number is 581-0379. Work is 228-3900.

BANK OFFICER: Please sign your name on this form. Now, how much do you want to deposit?

CARLA: I'll start with $250.00. Can you show me how to use my checking account?

BANK OFFICER: I'll be glad to. I'll show you how to write checks and how to deposit checks and cash. You'll also need to learn how to balance your checkbooks against your bank statement.

CARLA: Balance my checkbook?

BANK OFFICER: This is done by balancing what your statement says with what your checkbook says.

BANK OFFICER: Please have a seat. How can I help you today?

NANCY: We want to open an account here.

BANK OFFICER: What kind of account?

NANCY: Checking. We'd like to pay our bills without using cash or money orders.

BANK OFFICER: Would you also like to open a savings account?

NANCY: We'll wait to open a savings account until we have extra money to put away.

BANK OFFICER: Will this be two individual accounts or one joint account?

NANCY: A joint account. We both want to use the same account.

TOM: Is there a minimum balance here?

BANK OFFICER: Yes, sir. You must keep at least $5.00 in your account at all times. There is also a service charge of 10¢ for each check that you write.

TOM: Fine.

BANK OFFICER: How much do you plan to deposit?

NANCY: We're depositing our paychecks. They add up to $838.

BANK OFFICER: Very good. Please fill out this application form. I'll make the deposit if you will endorse these checks.

TOM: Just sign the backs of the checks?

BANK OFFICER: That's right.

TOM: Thanks for your help.

BANK OFFICER: My pleasure. And here are your temporary checks and your deposit receipt. Your printed checks will come in the mail in a couple of weeks.

PRACTICE USING THESE WORDS.
Find them in the conversations on page 4.
Write what they mean.   Write new sentences with them.

A.   to open an account   _____ to put money in the bank for the first time _____

_____ I opened an account at the bank on the corner. _____

B.   to reconcile a statement   _____

_____

C.   to have a seat   _____

_____

D.   to put money away   _____

_____

E.   to endorse a check   _____

_____

F.   to make a deposit   _____

_____

TALK TOPICS

A.   What is an individual account?   Did anyone on page 4 open an individual account?

B.   Why did Nancy and Tom open a joint account?

C.   What is the difference between a savings and a checking account?

D.   Why would you open a savings account? What kinds of savings accounts are there?

E.   Why did Tom and Nancy want to open a checking account?   What are some other advantages of a checking account?   What kinds of checking accounts are there?

F.   How do you deposit money in an account?

G.   How do you withdraw money from an account?

H.   What do you do if you have problems with your account?

I.   Does your bank charge you for each check you write?   How much? Do you pay a monthly service charge?

J.   What is a minimum balance?   Does your bank require one?

WHAT DO YOU SAY?
Practice with another student.   A customer is opening a new account at a bank.
Choose what you will say, line A or line B.   Only one line is the correct thing to say.

	BANK OFFICER	CUSTOMER
1.	**A.** Can I help you? **B.** What do you want?	**A.** I want to put money in this bank. **B.** I'd like to open an account here.

2.	A. OK, Mister. Checking or savings? B. Checking or savings?	A. Give me a checking account. B. I'd like a checking account.
3.	A. May I have your name, please? B. What's your name?	A. Roberto Sanchez. B. Roberto.
4.	A. And your address, Mr. Sanchez? B. Where do you live, Roberto?	A. On Evans Street. B. 9 Evans Street, Houston, Texas, 77027.
5.	A. May I have your Social Security number? B. Tell me your Social Security number.	A. It's 132-82-4000. B. It's 77027.
6.	A. When's your birthday? B. What is your birth date?	A. July 1, 1948. B. July 1.
7.	A. May I have the name, address, and phone number of your employer? B. Give me your boss's name, address, and phone number.	A. It's Carson's on Main. 750-1111. B. Bob Carson, Carson's Department Store, 45 Main Street, Houston, 77027, 750-1111.
8.	A. I'll need your home phone number. B. What's your number?	A. It's 770-9897. B. I told you.

FILL OUT THE APPLICATION.

A. Complete this application for Carla's checking account. One student asks for information and writes it on the form. The other student provides the information Carla gave the bank officer on page 4.

		Personal Account
☐ Checking ☐ Individual ☐ Savings ☐ Joint	Account Number	Date
Account Title CARLA DIMONA	Home Address (Include Zip Code)	
Signature X		
Social Security Number Date of Birth	Name and Address of Employer (Include Zip Code)	
Citizen of (Country) Birth Place	Home Telephone	Business Telephone

B. Practice giving information about yourself. Copy the account application form. One student asks for information and writes it on the form. The other student provides the information.

USING BANK FORMS

Practice filling out a deposit slip.
Nancy is depositing two checks into her checking account.
One check is for $43.25.   The other is for $75.42.

First Bank		Dollars	Cents
	CASH		
DATE	List Each Check 1		
	2		
FOR CREDIT TO THE ACCOUNT—PRINT FULL ACCOUNT TITLE (NAME)	3		
	4		
Checking Account Number	TOTAL		

Fill out this check.   It is for Nancy and Tom's June rent.
The rent is $400.00.   Make the check out to Raul Gomez.

TOM BROWN
NANCY BROWN

NO. 105

19

PAY TO THE
ORDER OF $

DOLLARS

People's Bank
1632 State St.
Shoreview, N.J. 08722

⑆023000326⑆ 026⑉ 229226 2⑈0105

Enter the deposit into Nancy and Tom's check register.
Then enter the check to Mr. Lopez.   Balance their checkbook.

ITEM NO. OR TRANSACTION CODE	DATE	DESCRIPTION OF TRANSACTION	AMOUNT OF PAYMENT OR WITHDRAWAL (−)		AMOUNT OF DEPOSIT (+)		BALANCE FORWARD	
		BE SURE TO DEDUCT FEES OR SERVICE CHARGES	**DEBITS**		**CREDITS**			
	5/17	TO FOR			838	00	838	00
103	5/20	TO Carson's Dept. Store FOR sweater	21	50			21	50
							816	50
104	5/27	TO Food World FOR groceries	40	00			40	00
							776	50
		TO FOR						
		TO FOR						

I'M SORRY, YOU CAN'T DO THAT

LISTEN TO THESE PEOPLE.
The bank employees are explaining the rules.

BANK GUARD: I'm sorry, but you'll have to go to the end of the line.
CUSTOMER: But I only have to make a quick deposit.
BANK GUARD: You still must wait in line. It's the rule.
CUSTOMER: I'm on my lunch hour. I'll never be through in time.
BANK GUARD: I understand, but other people are in a hurry too. It wouldn't be fair to them.
CUSTOMER: OK. I see your point. Next time I'll have to come at a different time.

CUSTOMER: Can you cash this check for me?
BANK TELLER: This is a "savings only" window. You can't cash checks here.
CUSTOMER: I know, but you're not busy. And I'm in a hurry.
BANK TELLER: I'd like to help. The problem is I don't have any cash at this window. I can only take deposits.
CUSTOMER: I see. I guess I'll have to go wait in line with everybody else.
BANK TELLER: I'm afraid so.

BANK TELLER: You don't have enough money in your account to cover this check.
CUSTOMER: That's impossible! I just deposited a check from my brother yesterday. I have a lot of money in my account.
BANK TELLER: That check hasn't cleared yet. It takes ten days for personal checks to clear. I'm afraid that's the rule.
CUSTOMER: Can't you make an exception just once?
BANK TELLER: No. I'm not allowed to make exceptions. I'll lose my job if I do.
CUSTOMER: All right. I guess I'll just have to wait until next week.

PRACTICE USING THESE WORDS.
Find them in the conversations on page 8.
Write what they mean.   Write new sentences with them.

A. to be through _____

_____

B. to see someone's point _____

_____

C. to cash a check _____

_____

D. to have enough to cover a check _____

_____

E. to have a check clear _____

_____

F. to make an exception _____

_____

WHAT DO YOU SAY?
Practice with another student.
A customer is at the checkout counter in a supermarket.
There are two possible conversations.
Listen to what the other student says.   Then, choose what you will say, line A or line B.

	CASHIER	CUSTOMER
1.	**A.** Do you have any sale coupons today? **B.** That'll be $25.00.	**A.** All right. Can I pay with a check? **B.** I've got a "$1.00 off" coupon for Wonder Wax.
2.	**A.** I'm sorry, but you can't use that coupon. That item isn't on sale anymore. **B.** We don't accept checks.	**A.** But I always cash checks in the other supermarket. **B.** Oh. I didn't look at the sale dates. Can't I use the coupon anyway?
3.	**A.** I'm afraid that you can't. All the sales are carefully planned. **B.** I'm sorry. Our rules are different. You'll have to pay in cash.	**A.** I don't have that much in cash. **B.** I see. Then I won't buy it today.

TRY IT IN CLASS.
Practice with another student.
One person is questioning the rules. Another person is explaining the rules.

Use expressions like these:

PERSON EXPLAINING RULE	PERSON NOT OBEYING RULE
I'm sorry, but . . .	I understand, but . . .
You're not allowed to . . .	I know, but . . .
You can't . . .	I see your point, but . . .
It's against the rules to . . .	Can't you make an exception . . .
You'll have to . . .	But I always . . .
You must . . .	What do you mean that . . .
I'm afraid that . . .	Why can't I . . .

A. A customer is trying to pay for something with a personal check.

MANAGER	CUSTOMER
1. tell store rule—no personal checks	1. you don't have enough money
2. suggest that customer use credit card	2. you don't have credit cards—ask manager to make exception
3. apologize, but say you can't make exception	3. you'll go to bank, cash check, and then come back to store

B. A customer is smoking in line at the bank.

BANK GUARD	CUSTOMER
1. tell bank rule—no smoking	1. you always smoke in bank
2. explain that smoking bothers many other customers	2. agree to put out cigarette

C. A customer is trying to bring a dog into a store.

MANAGER	CUSTOMER
1. tell store rule—no pets allowed	1. you're afraid to leave dog outside—it may get lost or stolen
2. explain that pets bother customers	2. offer to carry dog
3. agree to make exception	3. thank manager

D. A customer with over 20 items is in the "express line" of a supermarket. The cashier asks him/her to go to another line.

E. A customer wants to mail a package at the "stamps only" window in the Post Office. The clerk asks him/her to go to another window.

F. A person tries to put a dollar bill in the coin box on a bus. The bus driver tells the person that he/she needs exact change.

10

I'M SURE YOU'VE MADE A MISTAKE

LISTEN TO THESE PEOPLE.
One person is insisting that he/she is right.

CUSTOMER SERVICE: Can I help you?

YOKO: Yes. You sent me a late notice, and I've already paid my bill.

CUSTOMER SERVICE: Are you sure you paid it?

YOKO: Yes. I sent it out last week. I don't understand why you didn't get it.

CUSTOMER SERVICE: Did you send it to the right address?

YOKO: Yes. I used the pre-addressed envelope you sent with the bill. You should have gotten it by now.

CUSTOMER SERVICE: I'll check it. What's your name and account number?

YOKO: My name is Yoko Akiyama, A-K-I-Y-A-M-A. My account number is 567-34-891.

CUSTOMER SERVICE: Hold on, please. I'll see if we got it.

YOKO: I'll wait.

CUSTOMER SERVICE: Ms. Akiyama? I'm sorry for the inconvenience. We received your payment. The late notice was sent by mistake.

YOKO: That's all right. As long as you have it. Thanks for checking.

BANK OFFICER: Are you next?

FRED: Yes, I am. You've made a mistake on my statement.

BANK OFFICER: Are you certain?

FRED: I'm positive. I made a $300.00 deposit last month, and you didn't credit it to my account.

BANK OFFICER: Well, maybe you just think you made the deposit. Sometimes people forget.

FRED: No, I didn't forget. This is your mistake, not mine. Here's my copy of the deposit slip. This should have shown up on my statement.

BANK OFFICER: Oh. I'm sorry, Mr. Newman. This kind of thing doesn't happen often. I'll clear it up.

FRED: I should hope so. Make sure that it is added to my account this time.

TALK TOPICS

A. Talk about what Yoko said. Was she too polite?

B. Talk about what Fred said. Was he impolite?

C. How do you think Yoko would report a mistake on her bank statement? Would she act like Fred? Why? Why not?

D. Whose mistake do you think was more serious—the store's or the bank's?

E. What would you say if you were Yoko? if you were Fred?

11

Use expressions like these:

PERSON INSISTING	PERSON WITH DOUBTS
I'm certain . . .	Are you sure . . .
I'm positive . . .	Are you certain . . .
This (You) should have . . .	Maybe you . . .
I'm (pretty) sure . . .	Did you . . .
I don't understand why . . .	I'll see if . . .

A. A customer is returning a carton of sour milk to a store for a refund.

MANAGER	CUSTOMER
1. ask to help customer	1. you bought sour milk from this store—want refund
2. insist that milk is not from store—food here fresh	2. insist that you bought milk here; give manager receipt
3. say that customer *may* be right; apologize; agree to exchange	3. accept manager's apology

B. A doctor's receptionist tells a patient that the doctor is too busy to see him/her. The patient is insisting that he/she has an appointment.

RECEPTIONIST	PATIENT
1. doctor can't see patient; say office rule—must have appointment	1. you called yesterday and made appointment
2. ask if patient is certain about appointment; you don't have appointment on calendar	2. insist you're right
3. apologize and admit you made a mistake; offer to let patient see doctor next	3. accept apology

C. A customer is picking up a coat at the cleaner's and finds a stain on it.

CUSTOMER	MANAGER
1. there's a stain on your coat—it wasn't there before	1. insist stain was there before—it couldn't happen during cleaning
2. insist—no stain before; demand payment for damage	2. refuse to pay cost of replacing coat

D. A customer is complaining to Customer Service because he/she didn't receive the new television that he/she ordered.

E. A plumber is asking to be paid $15.00 for repair work on a sink drain. The customer insists that he/she only agreed to pay $10.00.

CALM DOWN, RELAX

LISTEN TO THESE PEOPLE.
One person is angry. The other person is trying to calm the angry person down.

OSCAR: I want to see the manager.

BANK OFFICER: He isn't here right now. Maybe I can help you.

OSCAR: He's never here when you need him. I'm fed up with all the mistakes you make around here.

BANK OFFICER: What's the problem?

OSCAR: You bounced my check to the telephone company, and I'm sure I have enough money in my account to cover it. I've had it with this bank!

BANK OFFICER: Please calm down. If you'll give me your account number and name, I'll look into this for you.

OSCAR: Don't tell me to calm down. Just straighten out this problem, or I'll take my business elsewhere.

BANK OFFICER: Won't you have a seat while I check this out? I'll be right back.

ANGELA: There's something wrong with this soup. It tastes sour.

WAITER: Really? No one else has complained about it.

ANGELA: Don't you think I can tell if the soup is sour or not? I don't care if no one else has complained. I'm telling you it's sour.

WAITER: Take it easy. I'll be glad to bring you something else. I'm sorry that you don't like the soup.

ANGELA: Well, you'd better tell the owner to throw away the rest of it before someone gets sick.

WAITER: I'll be sure to do that.

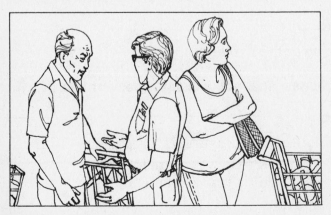

KWANG: Why do you only have one cashier working when the store is so crowded? We'll be here all night.

MANAGER: Don't get upset, please. I'll see what I can do.

KWANG: Don't tell me not to get upset. I'm tired, and I'm fed up with waiting in these long lines all the time.

MANAGER: I understand how you feel, sir. I'll have another cash register open in a minute.

PRACTICE USING THESE WORDS.
Find them in the conversations on page 13.
Write what they mean.   Write new sentences with them.

A.   to be fed up with _____

_____

B.   to bounce a check _____

_____

C.   to have had it with _____

_____

D.   to look into (something) _____

_____

E.   to take (your) business elsewhere _____

_____

F.   to check something out _____

_____

TALK TOPICS

A.   Why were Oscar, Angela, and Kwang angry?   Do you think they are right to be angry?
B.   What would you do if you were Oscar?   What would you do if you were Angela? What would you do if you were Kwang?
C.   Have you had similar experiences?
   Have you ever waited for a bus or train that was very late?
   Have you ever had a problem that your landlord wouldn't fix?
   Have you ever had an appliance fixed again and again?
   Have you ever been billed for something you didn't buy?
Did you get angry?   How did you show your anger?   What did you say?

WHAT DO YOU SAY?
Practice with another student.
A customer at a car repair service is complaining to the manager.
There are two possible conversations.
Listen to what the other student says.   Then choose what you will say, line A or line B.

	CUSTOMER	MANAGER
1.	**A.** I've had it with this station. **B.** Are you the manager? I'd like to talk to you.	**A.** Yes. How can I help you? **B.** What's the problem, sir?

2.	A.	I'm fed up with your mechanics. They can't do anything right.	A.	I understand how you could be upset. What haven't they been able to fix?
	B.	I've brought my car in for repairs three times this week. The mechanics haven't been able to fix it.	B.	Now calm down, sir. Please tell me exactly what's wrong with your car.
3.	A.	It leaks oil. If you can't get them to repair the leak, I'll take my business elsewhere.	A.	OK, take it easy. I'll check your car out myself. You're welcome to use one of our cars until yours is fixed.
	B.	It leaks oil. I'd hate to have to take my business to another station.	B.	I'll look into this right away. Please use one of our cars in the meantime. I'm sorry for the inconvenience.

TRY IT IN CLASS.
Practice with another student.
One person is angry. The other person is trying to calm the angry person down.

Use expressions like these:

ANGRY PERSON	PERSON CALMING OTHER PERSON
I'm fed up with . . .	Please calm down.
I'm upset about . . .	Maybe I can help you.
I've had it with . . .	Take it easy.
Don't tell me to . . .	I'll look into this.
You'd better straighten this out.	I'll check it out for you.

A. A customer is returning a damaged toaster.

CUSTOMER	SALES CLERK
1. ask to see manager	1. ask about problem; offer to help
2. angrily say that store sold you damaged toaster; you have exchanged it twice, and both those toasters were also damaged	2. try to calm customer; offer to exchange toaster again
3. you want money back	3. no refunds; can issue credit

B. A credit card customer is complaining about charges for things that he/she didn't buy. This is the third time this has happened.

CUSTOMER	CUSTOMER SERVICE
1. complain about company's service	1. ask about problem; offer to help
2. angrily state problem	2. try to calm customer; ask for customer's name and account number
3. refuse to be calmed; threaten to close your account	3. offer customer seat—you'll correct mistake

LOOK AT THE PICTURE.
Tell what each person is doing.

A. the man in the hat   <u>The man in the hat is opening a post office box.</u>

B. the woman next to the "all services" window _____

C. the woman at the "all services" window _____

D. the clerk at the "packages" window _____

E. the man at the "stamps" window _____

F. the man outside the window _____

HOW MUCH DOES IT COST?
You can buy these items at the post office. Write the cost next to each item.

ITEM	COST
air letter/aerogram	_____
postcard	_____
book of 20 stamps	_____
air mail stamp	_____
money order for $25.00	_____

LISTEN TO THESE PEOPLE.
The customer is asking the postal clerk for advice.

LAURA: Hi. Can you give me some advice? What's the best way to send a package to my brother in Japan?

CLERK: Well, you could send it either by Air Parcel Post or by Surface Parcel Post.

LAURA: Which do you recommend?

CLERK: Sending it by air is faster, of course. But then it's much more expensive.

LAURA: I want it to get there as soon as possible.

CLERK: Then I'd suggest sending it by air.

TRY IT IN CLASS.
Practice with another person.
One person asks for advice. The other person gives advice.

Use expressions like these:

ASKING FOR ADVICE	GIVING ADVICE
What do you advise?	I'd advise . . .
What do you suggest?	I'd suggest . . .
What do you recommend?	I'd recommend . . .
What would you do?	If I were you, I'd . . .

A. A customer wants to send an important letter. He wants to make sure that the person gets the letter. The postal clerk advises that the letter should be sent certified mail.

B. A customer wants to be sure that a letter gets someplace the next day. The postal clerk suggests sending it Express Mail.

C. A customer wants to send a package to California and doesn't want to spend a lot of money on postage. The postal clerk suggests sending it Fourth Class Mail.

SENDING PACKAGES

READ THESE MAILING TIPS FOR SENDING PACKAGES.
Use this information for the Talk Topics on page 19.

PACKAGE SERVICES FROM THE U.S. POSTAL SERVICE

Domestic Mail—You can send up to 70 pounds anywhere in the
continental United States. Packages may be sent by First Class
Mail (Priority Mail) or by Fourth Class Mail (Surface Parcel Post).
Fourth Class Mail is less expensive but is usually slower.

Overseas Mail—You must fill out a customs declaration form. You can
send packages by Air Parcel Post or by Surface Parcel Post. Air
Parcel Post is more expensive but is usually faster.

Express Mail—Delivery is guaranteed within 24 hours to most places
in the continental United States. Delivery to foreign countries
takes 48 hours or more. Express mail is more expensive than
Priority/First Class Mail.

OTHER SERVICES AVAILABLE AT EXTRA COST:

Insured Mail—You can insure packages up to $400.

Registered Mail—You can insure packages (usually cash, bonds, or
certificates of value) up to $25,000.

Certified Mail—A receipt is given to the sender when the post office
accepts the package. You may also ask for a Return Receipt
Requested form as proof that the addressee received the package.

UNITED PARCEL SERVICE (UPS)

UPS is a commercial carrier service that serves the United States and Canada.
- You can ship up to 50 pounds per package by UPS.
- Blue Label Air Service, which guarantees delivery within two days, is also
  available for an extra charge.
- All packages are automatically insured for $100.
- More insurance is available for an extra charge.

OTHER SERVICES BY AIR, TRAIN, AND BUS

- Train delivery is available through Amtrak Express Service.
- Bus delivery is available through Greyhound Package Express or
  Trailways Package Express.
- Delivery by air is available through Federal Express, Emery Express,
  and local airlines.

18

TALK TOPICS
Talk about sending packages. Use the information on page 18.

A. What is a customs declaration?

_____

B. What is the continental United States?

_____

C. Lee is sending a package to the Immigration and Naturalization Service. He wants to have proof that he mailed the package on a certain date. He also wants to have a receipt to be sure that the package was received. What should he ask for at the post office?

_____

D. Carmen is mailing a package of books to a friend. She doesn't want to spend too much on the postage. But if the books get lost or damaged, she wants to make sure she can replace them. What should she ask for at the post office?

_____

E. Mary wants to mail a present to her mother for her birthday next week. She wants to make sure that it gets there on time. Mary's mother lives in Haiti. What should Mary ask for at the post office? What must she fill out?

_____

F. Yung is sending some samples to a company in another state. It is very important that the package arrives at the other company the next day. What should Yung ask for at the post office?

_____

G. Bob wants to send a package to his sister in another state. First Class Mail is too expensive. What service should Bob use?

_____

H. Talk about your experiences with sending packages.
What kind of packages have you sent through the mail?
How did you send them? Did you insure the packages?
Did you use any of the other services? Which ones?

_____

POSSIBLY, PROBABLY, DEFINITELY

LISTEN TO THESE PEOPLE.
They are talking about how possible something is.

ALFREDO: If I mail this letter right now, will it get there by tomorrow?

POSTAL CLERK: Let's see. It's going to the next town. Yes. It'll probably get there by tomorrow.

ALFREDO: Is there a chance that it won't? I have to know for sure.

POSTAL CLERK: Well, there's a possibility that it won't. There's no guarantee if you send it by regular mail.

ALFREDO: I've heard about a service that guarantees delivery the next day.

POSTAL CLERK: Oh, you mean Express Mail. Yes, if you send the letter Express Mail, it'll definitely get there by tomorrow. It costs a lot more, though.

ALFREDO: That's all right. This letter must get there by tomorrow. I'll pay the extra money just to be sure.

KIM: Could you tell me if this package is wrapped well enough?

POSTAL CLERK: Let's see. It ought to hold up all right.

KIM: Do you think that the dishes inside could get damaged?

POSTAL CLERK: It's unlikely. If you packed them well, they'll probably be safe.

KIM: But it is possible that they could get damaged, isn't it?

POSTAL CLERK: Yes, there is a slight chance. Perhaps if you insure the package you'll feel better.

KIM: I guess I should get insurance. Then if something happens to the dishes, the insurance will pay for them.

PRACTICE USING THESE WORDS.
Find them in the conversations.
Write what they mean. Write new sentences with them.

A. to know for sure _____

_____

B. to hold up _____

_____

C. to guarantee delivery _____

_____

LOOK AT THESE WORDS.
The words on the left show that something is not possible (impossible).
The words on the right show that something is very possible or definite.
The words in the middle show that something is not definite but not impossible either.

impossible	unlikely	possible	probably	definitely
not possible	not likely	may/might	(most) likely	absolutely
can't	may not	a chance	should	will
won't	probably not	can/could		certainly
		perhaps		
		maybe		

TRY IT IN CLASS.
Practice with another student.
Talk about the possibility of something happening.

Use expressions like these:

There's a possibility that . . .	Perhaps/maybe
It's possible that . . .	Probably/most likely
There's a chance that . . .	Definitely/certainly
It's unlikely (not likely) that . . .	Possibly/may/might/could
It's not possible (impossible) . . .	Should/ought to/must

A. A customer is talking about the possibility of making an airplane reservation for a convenient time.

CUSTOMER	**TICKET AGENT**
1. you want a seat on the 6 P.M. flight to Puerto Rico; possible?	1. not possible—no seats left
2. possible to get later flight?	2. midnight flight is possible
3. midnight is too late—possible anyone will cancel reservation on 6:00 plane?	3. probable—usually happens; suggest that customer buy "stand-by" ticket

B. An employee is talking to his/her boss about the possibility of getting a raise.

EMPLOYEE	**EMPLOYER**
1. possible to talk to boss now?	1. yes, definitely; offer employee chair
2. possible to get raise soon?— haven't had one for a year	2. possible to get raise soon, but probably won't be a large raise
3. possible to get larger raise later in year?	3. not very possible—business is down

C. A patient is talking to a receptionist about the possibility of making a doctor's appointment for the evening.

PATIENT	RECEPTIONIST
1. ask for appointment with doctor —you want it for tomorrow night	1. doctor has no free time tomorrow night—he's free during day
2. say that you probably can't leave work during the day	2. it's possible that another patient will cancel appointment—then doctor will have time
3. ask how probable	3. tell how probable; offer to call patient if someone cancels

D. A tenant is talking to the landlord about the possibility of having some repairs made.

TENANT	LANDLORD
1. possible to have leaky faucet fixed today?	1. impossible—plumber on vacation
2. possible to use another plumber?	2. not possible to find another plumber
3. possible to have apartment painted?	3. impossible—but it is possible to get free paint; paint it yourself

E. A customer is talking to a clerk in a shoe repair store. The customer wants his/her shoes repaired by tomorrow. The clerk tells the customer that the store is very busy. They discuss the probability of having the shoes repaired in a day.

F. An employee is talking to the boss about the possibility of getting a promotion.

G. A customer is talking to a clerk about the possibility of getting the shirt that he/she likes in another size.

H. A tenant is talking to the landlord about the possibility of moving into a different apartment in the same building.

LOOK AT THIS ENVELOPE.
Answer the questions.

```
John Toledo
5 Westview Dr.
Boulder, CO 80303
```

```
        Sidney Walker
        2609 2nd Ave.
        Savannah, GA 31204
```

A. Who is sending this letter?
B. What is the sender's address?
C. Who is going to get this letter?
D. What is the zip code of the person who will get it?

ADDRESS THESE ENVELOPES.
You are the sender.

A. Send a letter to Ms. Sylvia Jacobs, who lives at
    884 Heather Drive in Westport, California.   Her zip code is 92734.

B. Send a letter to Mrs. Vera Stone, who lives at 5528 12th Ave., NW,
    in Naples, Florida.   Her zip code is 33999.

CLOSE-UP ON LANGUAGE

These four tenses can be used to talk about the present:

the present tense
She <u>works</u> downtown.

the present continuous tense
She <u>is working</u> now.

the present perfect tense
She <u>has worked</u> there for 3 years.

the present perfect continuous tense
She <u>has been working</u> since 9 o'clock.

THE PRESENT TENSE

You can use the present tense in the following types of sentences:

> We <u>eat</u> dinner at 6 o'clock.   It often <u>snows</u> in Vermont.
> These flowers <u>smell</u> nice.   The sweater <u>is</u> too small.
> July 4 <u>is</u> Independence Day.   The sun <u>sets</u> in the west.

For regular verbs, remember to add <u>s</u> when the subject is <u>she</u>, <u>he</u>, or <u>it</u> (or words that can replace <u>he</u>, <u>she</u>, or <u>it</u>).
Study the forms of the irregular verbs <u>be</u> and <u>have</u>.

A. I _____ am _____ tired.   (to be)

B. They _____ open until 9 on Thursdays.   (to stay)

C. That shirt _____ long sleeves, doesn't it?   (to have)

D. I _____ a headache.   (to have)

E. We _____ very hungry.   (to be)

F. The sun _____ almost every day here.   (to shine)

G. I _____ coffee at breakfast.   (to drink)

H. The bank _____ at 8:30 in the morning.   (to open)

I. Carlos _____ an old car.   (to drive)

J. You _____ Chinese food, don't you?   (to like)

K. This blanket _____ nice and soft.   (to feel)

L. Maria _____ in the hospital.   (to be)

M. The students _____ around and talk before class.   (to stand)

N. You _____ from Japan.   (to be)

O. We _____ together at parties.   (to dance)

THE PRESENT CONTINUOUS TENSE

You can use the present continuous tense in the following types of sentences:

They <u>are watching</u> TV right now.   He <u>is being</u> stubborn.
I <u>am writing</u> to Fred while he's away.   She <u>is jogging</u> on the weekends.

Notice that this tense is formed with <u>be</u> + <u>verb</u> + <u>-ing</u>.

FILL IN THE MISSING WORDS.
Use the present continuous tense of the verb in parentheses.

A. Bill _____ is walking _____ home.   (to walk)

B. We _____ for the doctor.   (to wait)

C. They _____ to school on Thursday evenings.   (to go)

D. I _____ a letter to my friend.   (to write)

E. Ron _____ a girl he met at the beach.   (to date)

F. It _____.   (to rain)

G. Peter and I _____ the bus to work this week.   (to take)

H. You _____ late tonight, aren't you?   (to work)

I. Nancy and Tom _____ at my house.   (to stay)

J. They _____ a new house across the street.   (to build)

K. I _____ the Sunday newspaper.   (to read)

L. She _____ up earlier in the mornings.   (to get)

M. We _____ about where to go for dinner.   (to talk)

N. I _____ a package to my sister.   (to mail)

O. You _____ sick, aren't you?   (to feel)

THE PRESENT PERFECT TENSE

You can use the present perfect tense in the following types of sentences:

They <u>have eaten</u> already.   She <u>has had</u> a cold this month.
We <u>have driven</u> home this week.   It <u>has rained</u> a lot recently.
You <u>have lived</u> there for months. She <u>has been</u> on a diet since Tuesday.

Notice that this tense is formed with <u>have</u> + past participle.
Remember that the past participle of irregular verbs is <u>not</u> formed by adding <u>-ed</u>.

FILL IN THE MISSING WORDS.
Use the present perfect tense of the verb in parentheses.

A. Sam ___<u>has worked</u>___ all of his life.   (to work)

B. We _____ the bus again.   (to miss)

C. She _____ sick for two weeks.   (to be)

D. They _____ at this restaurant many times.   (to eat)

E. I _____ you ten times in the last two hours.   (to call)

F. He _____ sick since this morning.   (to feel)

G. We _____ each other once a week for the past year.   (to see)

H. Dan _____ the piano since he was twelve.   (to play)

I. You _____ better since your vacation.   (to look)

J. They _____ in that house ever since I've known them.   (to live)

K. It _____ every weekend this month.   (to rain)

L. Our family _____ this dog since it was a puppy.   (to have)

M. The sky _____ cloudy again.   (to turn)

N. He _____ a lot of work today.   (to do)

O. This building _____ here for a hundred years.   (to stand)

P. I _____ this painting ever since I first saw it.   (to love)

Q. We _____ the bus to work every day this week.   (to take)

R. My arm _____ since I bruised it.   (to hurt)

THE PRESENT PERFECT CONTINUOUS TENSE

You can use the present perfect continuous tense in the following types of sentences:

They have been working since noon.   She has been sleeping all day.
I have been looking for an apartment.   He has been driving to class.

Notice that this tense is formed with have + been + verb + -ing.

FILL IN THE MISSING WORDS.
Use the present perfect continuous tense of the verb in parentheses.

A. Jose _____ has been cooking _____ all day.   (to cook)

B. We _____ to this restaurant since it opened.   (to come)

C. It _____ all day and all night.   (to rain)

D. You _____ TV all evening.   (to watch)

E. They _____ on the phone for hours.   (to talk)

F. We _____ to work.   (to walk)

G. I _____ for you since twelve o'clock.   (to wait)

H. She _____ the same book for a month.   (to read)

I. Tom _____ since he was sixteen.   (to smoke)

J. The phone _____ all day.   (to ring)

K. I _____ for two years.   (to jog)

L. He _____ better lately.   (to sleep)

M. They _____ their money for a new car.   (to save)

N. You _____ for three hours already.   (to drive)

O. The fire _____ since this morning.   (to burn)

REVIEW THE PRESENT TENSES.
Rewrite the sentences. Use the new subjects given.

A. Fred has been looking for you. Fred and I ___have been looking for you___.

B. They have gone to the post office. He _____.

C. We ride the train every day. Carla _____.

D. The bank is open on Saturdays. The stores _____.

E. I have read the newspaper today. Lin _____.

F. We have been shopping for groceries. He _____.

G. The customer is filling out forms. The customers _____.

H. You have answered my question. He _____.

I. He studies too hard. You _____.

J. We are planning a party. Rick _____.

K. They have been waiting for you since noon. He _____.

L. She likes yogurt. We _____.

M. They are talking on the phone. He _____.

N. He is busy. I _____.

O. They have been running daily. Betty _____.

P. He owns a small house. They _____.

Q. I have been living on Pine Street. He _____.

R. I have been upset. Lee _____.

S. Alfredo and I are building a shed. Alfredo _____.

T. You seem sick. Don _____.

U. We are selling the car. She _____.

V. He remembers you. I _____.

W. I have been depositing money in the bank. Lan _____.

X. They have bought a new TV. Maria _____.

Y. We practice English at home. He _____.

Z. She is meeting him at the train station. They _____.

28

NEGATIVES

Present Tense

The toaster works.   The toaster <u>does not</u> (<u>doesn't</u>) work.

We eat vegetables.   We <u>do not</u> (<u>don't</u>) eat vegetables.

I am late.   I <u>am not</u> late.

Rita is here.   Rita <u>is not</u> (<u>isn't</u>) here.

They are home.   They <u>are not</u> (<u>aren't</u>) home.

Present Continuous Tense

He is coming with us.   He <u>is not coming</u> with us.

We are working.   We <u>are not working</u>.

Present Perfect Tense

She has called.   She <u>has not</u> (<u>hasn't</u>) called.

They have eaten.   They <u>have not</u> (<u>haven't</u>) eaten.

Present Perfect Continuous Tense

It has been raining.   It <u>has not been raining</u>.

I have been waiting.   I <u>have not been waiting</u>.

REWRITE THESE SENTENCES.
Use the negative.

A. I think you're right. _____ I don't think you're right. _____ .

B. You are studying very hard. _____ .

C. She has called me recently. _____ .

D. We have been going to class. _____ .

E. These sweaters are on sale. _____ .

F. I am visiting them tonight. _____ .

G. They have been out all day. _____ .

H. It is snowing. _____ .

I. You are talking too much. _____ .

J. We have eaten. _____ .

K. This line is moving very quickly. _____ .

L. The door is open. _____ .

M. I have been smoking. _____ .

N. I have paid the bill. _____ .

O. We want dinner now. _____ .

P. Rita plays the piano. _____ .

Q. I have been saving money. _____ .

R. They have met before. _____ .

QUESTIONS

Present Tense

Does he work here?
Do you live on 8th Street?
Am I late?
Is Kim here?
Are they all right?

Present Continuous Tense

Is it raining?
Are you watching that TV program?

Present Perfect Tense

Has the doctor seen you yet?
Have you been here before?

Present Perfect Continuous Tense

Has the phone been ringing all day?
Have they been looking for me?

WRITE QUESTIONS.

A. __Are you waiting for the doctor__ ? Yes, I'm waiting for the doctor.

B. _____ ? No, Fred hasn't opened a bank account.

C. _____ ? Yes, I'm tired.

D. _____ ? No, he hasn't been waiting a long time.

E. _____ ? Yes, I've seen the new movie.

F. _____ ? No, we haven't met each other before.

G. _____ ? Yes, we are ready.

H. _____ ? No, they haven't been saving their money.

I. _____ ? Yes, you have been sitting in my seat.

J. _____ ? No, Carla doesn't walk to work.

K. _____ ? Yes, I have been reading that book.

L. _____ ? No, the rain hasn't started again.

M. _____ ? Yes, Anna has been writing to Carlos.

N. _____ ? No, the restaurant is not open tonight.

O. _____ ? Yes, Oscar is looking for a job.

P. _____ ? No, you and Maria aren't too late.

Q. _____ ? Yes, they know how to drive.

R. _____ ? No, I'm not talking on the phone.

30

NEGATIVE QUESTIONS

Present Tense

Doesn't she <u>work</u> here anymore?
Don't you <u>want</u> to eat something?
Isn't it a nice day?
Aren't you hungry?

Present Continuous Tense

Isn't he <u>coming</u> over?
Aren't you <u>talking</u> to each other?

Present Perfect Tense

Hasn't the rain <u>stopped</u> yet?
Haven't you <u>seen</u> enough?

Present Perfect Continuous Tense

Hasn't he been <u>talking</u> for hours?
Haven't they <u>been working</u> since this morning?

WRITE QUESTIONS.
Use the negative.

A. ___Isn't the store open late tonight___ ? No, the store isn't open late tonight.

B. _____ ? Yes, we've been here before.

C. _____ ? No, she's not sitting in my chair.

D. _____ ? Yes, we've spoken together before.

E. _____ ? No, they haven't been staying in a hotel.

F. _____ ? Yes, the mailman has come already.

G. _____ ? No, the bank's not closed.

H. _____ ? Yes, she is waiting for the manager.

I. _____ ? No, I don't have a car.

J. _____ ? Yes, I'm next.

K. _____ ? No, he hasn't been sick.

L. _____ ? Yes, I'm going to the party tonight.

M. _____ ? No, he's not working tomorrow.

N. _____ ? Yes, the TV is on.

O. _____ ? No, you haven't got the flu.

P. _____ ? Yes, they have been listening to the radio.

Q. _____ ? No, she hasn't been writing to Anna.

UNIT 2

I KNOW YOU'LL LOVE THIS CAR

IN THIS UNIT, YOU WILL BE:

responding to sales pressure
talking about how much you like or don't
    like something
reading and telephoning about used car
    ads in newspapers
bargaining for a good price
talking about the documents you need to
    own and drive a car
asking for favors and telling people you
    will do a favor for them
asking people if they have remembered or
    have forgotten to do something
complaining and showing annoyance

In the Close-Up on Language, you will
review:

the verb forms you use to talk about and
    ask about things that happened in the
    past (simple past, past continuous,
    past perfect, past perfect continuous)
the verb forms you use to talk about and
    ask about things that will happen in
    the future

LOOK AT THE PICTURE.
Find these things in the picture.

1. engine/motor
2. tires
3. hood
4. steering wheel
5. headlight

6. windshield
7. bumper
8. rear-view mirror
9. van
10. sports car

TALK TOPICS

LOOK AT THE PICTURE.
Talk about what you see.

What is this place?
What can you buy here?
What do the signs mean?

Why is the man looking at the engine?
Why is the woman sitting in the driver's
    seat?
Why are some of the people leaving?
What do you think the salespeople and
    the customers are talking about?

Do you own a car?
Where did you buy it?
Did you ever go to a used car lot?
What were the salespeople like?

Cars are an important part of life in the
    United States. Are they as important
    in your native country?
Did you own a car in your native country?
Did you need a car there?

Pretend to be one of the people in the
    picture. What were you doing in the
    picture on page 33? What are you
    doing now? What are you saying?
Which car do you want to buy? Why?
    What don't you like about the other
    cars? How much do you want to
    pay? Will you pay the price written
    on the car?

34

ASK QUESTIONS ABOUT THE PICTURE.
Write down the new words and expressions you want to remember.

11. _____   16. _____
12. _____   17. _____
13. _____   18. _____
14. _____   19. _____
15. _____   20. _____

RESPONDING TO SALES PRESSURE

LISTEN TO THESE PEOPLE.
The salespeople are using sales pressure.   The customers are not ready to buy.

SALESMAN: Good afternoon.   What can I do for you today?

ROBERTO: I'm looking for a car that gets good mileage.

SALESMAN: I've got just the car for you. This one just came in today.   It gets an incredible 32 miles to the gallon.

ROBERTO: That is good!   But I'm afraid that the price is too high for me.

SALESMAN: Don't let the price stand in your way.   I can arrange a monthly payment plan that's just right for your budget. You can take two years to pay it off. And think of the money you'll save on gas.

ROBERTO: It all sounds very good, but I don't know.   I really don't want to spend that much.

SALESMAN: Tell you what.   Why don't you take it for a test drive?   You'll love the way this car handles.

ROBERTO: I'll have to think about it. Besides, I don't have time for a test drive today.

SALESMAN: You really shouldn't pass this one by.   It might not be here tomorrow.

ROBERTO: I'll have to take that chance.   I want to shop around some more.

SALESMAN: OK.   Let me give you my card. Just give me a call if you change your mind.   But don't take too long.

ROBERTO: Thanks.   I'll keep it in mind.

SALESWOMAN: How are you today?   Can I help you with something?

MIKE: I'm looking for a reliable car.   Nothing fancy.

SALESWOMAN: OK.   Let me get a little information.   Do you have a trade in?

MIKE: No, I don't.   This will be my first car.

SALESWOMAN: I see.   And how much did you want to spend?

MIKE: I'd like to stay under $2,000.

SALESWOMAN: I think I have the perfect car for you.   For $500 down and $150 a month for two years, this little beauty can be yours.

MIKE: Well, it looks kind of old.

SALESWOMAN: It's only six years old, and it only has 23,000 miles on it.

MIKE: Haven't you got something newer?

SALESWOMAN: Not for this price.   Why don't you get in and turn the engine over?   You won't believe how well it runs.

MIKE: I'm sure it does, but this isn't exactly what I had in mind.   I'll have to think it over.

SALESWOMAN: Take your time.   But you're not going to find a deal like this anywhere else in town.

MIKE: Well, thanks for your help.   I'll let you know what I decide.

SALESWOMAN: My name is Candy Jones. Just ask for me.

MIKE: OK.   Bye now.

PRACTICE USING THESE WORDS.
Find them in the conversations on page 36.
Write what they mean. Write new sentences with them.

A. let (something) stand in your way _____

_____

B. to pay it off _____

_____

C. pass (something) by _____

_____

D. to shop around _____

_____

E. to change your mind _____

_____

F. to keep it in mind _____

_____

G. to have in mind _____

_____

TALK TOPICS

A. What is sales pressure? Has anyone ever pressured you to buy
something? What did you do?
B. Why do people buy used cars?
C. Which is cheaper, a new car or a used car?
D. Where can you buy a used car? Where can you buy a new car?
E. What is a trade-in? What is a down payment? How do these
things change what you pay for a car?
F. Roberto put money in a savings account until he had enough money to
pay the full price for a car. Mike bought his car by getting a loan
from the bank. Mike paid the bank a monthly payment every month
for two years until the loan was paid back. How would you buy a car? Why?
G. How can you find out which new cars are the best?
H. How can you find out if a used car is in good condition?
I. Why is it important to know about a car's gas mileage?
J. What other information should you have about a car before you buy?

WHAT DO YOU SAY?
Practice with another student. Choose what you will say, line A or line B.
Only one line is the correct thing to say.

	SALESPERSON		CUSTOMER
1.	A.	Can I help you?	A. I don't know. What do you have?
	B.	What do you want?	B. I'm looking for a sportscar.
2.	A.	How about this van?	A. Looks great, but the price is too high for me.
	B.	This one is just the car for you.	B. This price isn't what I had in mind.
3.	A.	Don't let that stand in your way. I can arrange a loan.	A. I don't want it.
	B.	How about a loan?	B. Thanks, but I don't think so.
4.	A.	Why not take it for a test drive? You'll fall in love with it.	A. I'm sure I would, but I really can't afford it.
	B.	You'll be sorry. You really should buy it.	B. I'll keep it in mind.
5.	A.	Shop around. You'll change your mind.	A. Thanks. I'll think it over.
	B.	Well, here's my card. Call me if you change your mind.	B. I don't think so.

TRY IT IN CLASS.
Practice with another student.
The salesperson should use sales pressure.
The customer should not agree to buy.

Use expressions like these:

SALESPEOPLE	CUSTOMERS
This is just the . . . for you	I don't know.
You really should/shouldn't . . .	I don't think so.
You'll love . . .	I'll keep it in mind.
You won't believe . . .	I'll think it over.
Don't let the price stand in your way.	I'll let you know.
I can arrange . . . payment plan.	This isn't what I had in mind.
You're not going to find . . .	I'm afraid that . . .
Call me if you change your mind.	I'd like to shop around.

A. There is a sale on TVs, and a customer is looking at them.

SALESPERSON	CUSTOMER
1. offer to help	1. you want to look at color TVs
2. show one for $1200; describe it	2. you don't want to spend that much

3. try to get customer to pay for it with time payments

4. you don't have anything for $400; try to get customer to use cash as a down payment on more expensive TV

3. you don't want to use credit; you have $400 cash and don't want to spend more

4. be firm; you like the TV, but you know you can't spend that much

B. The customer is looking at bedroom furniture in a department store.

SALESPERSON	CUSTOMER
1. offer to help	1. you are looking for a double bed
2. show customer a bedroom set with bed, dresser, two night stands, and two lamps; describe them	2. you didn't plan on spending that much; you only want the bed
3. you want to sell the whole set; use sales pressure	3. you like it, but you can't afford to buy it all
4. offer easy payment plan	4. you don't think you should use credit; you want time to think it over

C. Cut out advertisements from the newspaper or a magazine and bring them to class. Try to sell the item in the ad to another student. Use sales pressure.

DO YOU LIKE IT?

LISTEN TO THESE PEOPLE.
They are talking about how much one person likes or dislikes something.

SALESPERSON: What kind of car are you looking for?
KIM: I want a small car that gets good mileage.
SALESPERSON: What do you think about this one?
KIM: It's not bad. I'm not sure that it's for me though.
SALESPERSON: Well, then I think you'll find this four-door sedan more to your liking.
KIM: It is closer to what I had in mind. But I'm still not wild about it.
SALESPERSON: Please look around. Is there something that interests you?
KIM: Yes! That red convertible looks great! It's just the car I've always dreamed about.

SALESPERSON: How do you like this car? It's a beauty, isn't it?

ROBERTO: It's all right. I'm not crazy about it though.

SALESPERSON: Perhaps this sportscar is more your style.

ROBERTO: That's more like it. I like that one a lot.

SALESPERSON: Would you like to try sitting in it?

ROBERTO: Yes, I would. Thanks.

SALESPERSON: Isn't this a terrific looking car?

MIKE: Not really. I hate big cars.

SALESPERSON: Oh. Then I'll bet you'll be wild about that green two-door sedan.

MIKE: It's OK. But I don't care for the color. Now, that brown van looks fantastic.

SALESPERSON: Would you be interested in taking a better look at it?

MIKE: I certainly would.

WHAT DO YOU SAY?
Practice with another student. There are two possible conversations.
Listen to what the other student says. Then, choose what you will say, line A or line B.

	SALESPERSON	CUSTOMER
1.	A. This stereo is beautiful, isn't it? B. This stereo is OK, isn't it?	A. I love it, but it looks expensive. B. I'm not crazy about it.
2.	A. We can work out a payment plan that's right for your budget. B. Perhaps this one is more your style.	A. That's more like it. B. I'm not crazy about using credit. Let me think it over.

	SALESPERSON	CUSTOMER
1.	A. What do you think of this leather jacket? B. Can I interest you in a leather jacket?	A. No. I don't care for leather. B. I love it, but I'm not sure that it's for me.
2.	A. It will look great on you. Would you like to try it on? B. Please look around. Maybe something else will interest you.	A. I certainly would. B. All right. I'll let you know if I see anything I like.

TRY IT IN CLASS.
Practice with another student.
The salespeople are asking how the customers like something.
The customers are responding to the questions.

Use expressions like these:

SALESPEOPLE	CUSTOMERS
Do you like this . . .	I love . . .
How do you like this . . .	It's great/fantastic/terrific
Isn't this . . .	. . . just what I've always dreamed about
What do you think about . . .	like . . . a lot
How do you feel about . . .	It's OK/all right/not bad
Can I interest you in . . .	I'm not wild about/crazy about
Would you be interested in . . .	I'm not sure that it's for me
Would you like . . .	It's not what I had in mind
	It's not my style
	I don't care for . . .
	I hate . . .

A. The customer is looking in a department store.

SALESPERSON	CUSTOMER
1. try to sell a red wool sweater	1. give your opinion—be negative
2. try to sell a white orlon	2. give your opinion—you hate white
3. try to sell a blue cashmere	3. give your opinion—you want it, but you can't afford it
4. try to sell a green cotton	4. give your opinion—you'll buy it

B. The customer is looking for a book to read.

SALESPERSON	CUSTOMER
1. try to sell a murder mystery	1. give your opinion—be negative
2. try to sell a love story	2. give your opinion—not interested
3. try to sell a science fiction book	3. give your opinion—you want it

C. Bring mail-order catalogues to class. Talk about the things you like in the catalogue. Talk about the things you don't like.

D. Talk about other things you like or don't like:
1. movies—favorite or least favorite movies, actors, directors
2. books—favorite or least favorite books, authors
3. food—favorite or least favorite foods or restaurants
4. music—favorite or least favorite songs and singers

BUYING FROM THE NEWSPAPER

LOOK AT THESE NEWSPAPER ADS.
They are for used cars. Use them to answer the questions below.

CHEVY NOVA 4-DR 1979
6-cyl. sedan with a/c. Body/interior like new. Exc. cond. Snow tires. Orig. owner. $3,675. 971-6984

'76 DATSUN B-210
38 MPG. Orig. ownr. 48,000 mi. AM-FM Heater. 4-spd. W/W tires. Mint showrm. cond. $2,600. 9 am–10 pm. 243-5666

DODGE ASPEN '79 STATION WAGON
6-cyl, auto. trans., excl. running cond., PB, PS. New radials. Gd. mpg. Must sell. $2975. Call 621-9147

'75 FORD MUSTANG
Auto., 4-cyl., PS. Radio w/ 8-track. Blue with white vinyl roof. 51,000 mi. No dents, rust. $2,175. 564-0689

1974 MAZDA
6-cyl. autom., PS, PB, AM-FM stereo, many new parts. Very good running condition. $1400. 221-3644

OLDS STA WGN '79 Dsl
Loaded w/extras. Immac. cond. New brakes. $4500 or best offer. 783-4939 days; 234-5786 eves.

'71 PONTIAC LE MANS
4-dr., auto. trans., PS, PB. Good transportation. Priced to sell. $575. Call 423-6592.

'74 VW DASHER
4-spd, am/fm, R/defog, new tires. Exc. cond. thruout, gar. kept. $1,850. Call 618-3137

TALK TOPICS

A. The ads use many abbreviations. What do these abbreviations mean?

4-dr. _____	mpg. _____	gd. _____
cyl. _____	mi. _____	dsl. _____
a/c _____	W/W tires _____	eves. _____
exc. _____	auto. trans. _____	spd. _____
cond. _____	PB	gar. _____
orig. _____	PS _____	

B. What are the "new radials" in the Dodge Aspen ad?
C. What is the "8-track" in the Ford Mustang ad?
D. What is the meaning of "best offer" in the Olds station wagon ad?
E. You want to call about the Olds station wagon. It's 2:00 in the afternoon. What phone number do you call?
F. It's 8:30 in the morning. Can you call about the Datsun B-210?
G. Which do you like better, automatic or standard (manual) transmission? Why?
H. Which car is the most expensive? Which one is the least expensive?
I. Which car would you call about? Why?

LISTEN TO THESE PEOPLE.
Pat is the owner of the Oldsmobile station wagon in the ad on page 42.
Marta is calling Pat about the ad.

MARTA: Hello. I'm calling about the
    Oldsmobile station wagon.
PAT: Yes. What would you like to know?
MARTA: How many miles does it have on it?
PAT: Only 30,000. It's in excellent
    condition. I've never had any trouble
    with it.
MARTA: What about the gas mileage?
PAT: Well, you know it's a diesel. I get about
    25 miles per gallon. That's good for a
    car this size.
MARTA: Does it have air conditioning?
PAT: Yes, it does. Also power steering and
    power brakes.
MARTA: The price seems kind of high.
    Would you be willing to take less?
PAT: Why don't you take a look at it and
    make me an offer?
MARTA: OK. Let's see. Tomorrow is Friday,
    and I'm busy this weekend. How about
    Monday evening?
PAT: I wouldn't wait that long if I were you.
    A few other people are coming to look at
    it this weekend.
MARTA: I see. Well, how about this evening
    at 7?
PAT: Fine. Let me give you the address.

TRY IT IN CLASS.
Practice with another student.

A. Choose an ad from the ones on page 42. What questions would you ask?
    Use the following example to get started:

BUYER	SELLER
1. you are calling about Chevy Nova	1. ask what buyer wants to know
2. number of miles on car?	2. make up a number
3. gas mileage?	3. make up a number
4. ask to see the car	4. say when buyer can see it; give your address

B. Look at the ads in your newspaper.
    Look at ads for cars, pets, services, etc.
    Pick an ad you would call. Tell what questions you would ask.
    Tell what you like about the ad.

BARGAINING FOR A GOOD PRICE

LISTEN TO THESE PEOPLE.
Rick and Fred are trying to agree on a price.

FRED: Well, what do you think? Isn't it in great shape?

RICK: Not bad. There are a couple of problems here and there. What did you say you wanted for it?

FRED: The asking price is $4500. It's worth every penny of it.

RICK: That's more than I wanted to spend. $4500 is a little steep. Would you consider taking less?

FRED: What did you have in mind?

RICK: I was thinking about $3500. That's even more than I can afford. And the car's going to need a new muffler soon.

FRED: The muffler will hold up for at least another 10,000 miles. I'm sure of it. Look, I can let it go for $4200, but not a penny less.

RICK: I'm afraid that I can't come up with that much. Maybe I can stretch my budget to $3750. But that's my final offer.

FRED: What do you say we split the difference? I want to close this deal today and get it off my mind. Give me $4000 even, and we've got a deal.

RICK: Oh, I don't know! $4000 seems like an awful lot of money. I'll have to think it over.

FRED: What's there to think over? You know $4000 is a steal for this car. Other people are coming to look at it later. It'll be sold by tomorrow.

RICK: I'll have to take my chances. I don't like to make hasty decisions. I'd like to sleep on it. I'll call you in the morning.

FRED: You really drive a hard bargain. Tell you what. Give me a check for $3800 and it's yours.

RICK: You mean it? Well . . . all right. Gee, I hope I won't regret this.

FRED: Don't worry. You won't be sorry. The car has a lot of life left in it.

RICK: I sure hope so. Let's get on with it before I change my mind.

PRACTICE USING THESE WORDS.
Find them in the conversation on this page.
Write what they mean. Write new sentences with them.

A. to be in great shape _____

_____

B. to hold up _____

_____

C. to let it go for (price) _____

_____

D. to come up with (money) _____

_____

E. to split the difference _____

_____

F. to close a deal _____

_____

G. to take your chances _____

_____

H. to sleep on it _____

_____

I. to drive a hard bargain _____

_____

J. to get on with it _____

_____

TALK TOPICS

A. What can you bargain for in the United States?
Can you bargain for a house? your salary at work? auto repairs?

B. Where is it all right to bargain? Where is it not all right?
Can you bargain in a department store? in a supermarket?
at a flea market? at a car dealer's? with someone who is selling
something he owns?

C. Have you ever bargained for something? Talk about your experiences.

D. Do people in your native country bargain more or less than they do in the U.S.?

TRY IT IN CLASS.
Practice with another student.
Try to sell something you own: car, bike, house, clothing, etc.
Bargain until you both agree to a price.

CAR DRIVERS AND THE LAW

If you own and drive a car, you must have the following:

- a driver's license or learner's permit
- a registration certificate showing ownership
- license plates
- insurance

Your state may also require you to have your car inspected. If the inspector says your car is safe to drive, you will get a safety inspection sticker.

Laws are different in different states. Talk about the laws in your state.

Use expressions like these:

You have to	You don't have to
You must	
You need	You don't need to
The law requires you to	The law doesn't require you to

A. Do you own a car? Do you have proof that you are the owner? What can happen if you don't have proof?

B. Do you have a driver's license? What did you have to do to get your license? What kinds of tests did you have to take?

C. What is the difference between a driver's license and a learner's permit?

D. Not all states require you to have license plates on both the front and the back of your car. What is the law in your state?

E. What kind of insurance does your state require you to have? What kind of insurance do you think you should have?

F. Do cars have to be inspected in your state?

G. Who issues driver's licenses, registration certificates, and license plates? Where do you have to go to get them?

H. How much do you have to pay for a driver's license? a registration certificate? license plates?

I. What may happen if you drive without a license? if you drive without license plates? if you drive without enough insurance?

J. What documents are required in your native country?

K. Talk about other laws about driving:
1. speed limits
2. driving and drinking
3. meeting a stopped school bus
4. traffic lights and signs
5. parking
6. yielding to emergency vehicles (police cars, ambulances, fire trucks)
7. littering
8. emissions control devices

ASKING FOR FAVORS

LISTEN TO THESE PEOPLE.
One person is asking for a favor.

BETTY: Excuse me. I'm very sorry to bother you at this time of night.

PETER: That's OK. What's the problem?

BETTY: I've got a flat tire and no jack. I was wondering if I could use your phone to call a tow truck.

PETER: Sure. Come right in. The telephone's over there. Where did you leave your car?

BETTY: At the top of the hill. I hope you don't mind that I rang your bell. I didn't know where else to turn.

PETER: Forget it. It's no problem. I've got a jack you could borrow.

BETTY: Oh, that's very nice of you. That would save me the expense of a tow truck.

PETER: Look. I'll give you a hand with the tire. It's too hard to do it alone in the dark.

BETTY: I'd hate to make you go out of your way like that.

PETER: Don't worry about it. I'm glad to help. Just let me get the jack and a flashlight.

BETTY: I really appreciate your kindness. I feel bad about your going to so much trouble.

PETER: It's no trouble. Really. Let's go.

RICK: Hey, Mike. Are you in a big hurry?

MIKE: Kind of. Carla's making dinner for me tonight. Why? What's up?

RICK: I hate to hold you up, but do you think you could give me a boost? My battery is dead.

MIKE: Of course. Do you have booster cables?

RICK: I'm afraid not. Don't you have a set?

MIKE: Yes, but they're at home in the garage. Listen, I'll drive home and get them. I'll be right back.

RICK: I'm sorry to bother you like this. I hope you don't mind.

MIKE: That's all right. What are friends for?

RICK: Mike, as long as you're going home anyway, would you mind doing me another favor?

MIKE: Sure, what is it?

RICK: Would you bring back the sweater you borrowed from me?

MIKE: Sure. I'll see you in a few minutes.

RICK: OK. Thanks again.

PRACTICE USING THESE WORDS.
Find them in the conversations on page 47.
Write what they mean. Write new sentences with them.

A. not know where to turn _____

_____

B. give someone a hand _____

_____

C. go out of your way _____

_____

D. go to so much (this much) trouble _____

_____

E. hold someone up _____

_____

F. as long as you're going _____

_____

WHAT DO YOU SAY?
Practice with another student. Pretend you don't know the other student.
You need someone to help you push your car to a garage.
Choose what you will say, line A or line B. Only one line is the correct thing to say.

	PERSON #1	**PERSON #2**
1.	A. Excuse me. Could you help me? B. Hey. I need some help.	A. Sure. What's the problem? B. What do you want?
2.	A. I'm sorry to bother you, but my car won't start. B. I was wondering if you could start my car.	A. Don't worry about it. B. Is the battery dead? I could give you a boost.
3.	A. I feel bad about asking you to push me to the garage. B. I don't think it's the battery. I'm afraid I need a push to the garage.	A. No problem. I'd be happy to give you a push. B. I don't care if you need help.
4.	A. I don't know where else to turn. Thank you. B. I hate to make you go to so much trouble. I really appreciate your kindness.	A. I really don't mind. I'm going that way anyway. B. Of course. It's too hard to do it alone.

TRY IT IN CLASS.
Practice with another student.

Read the situations at the bottom of this page. For each situation, ask the other student for the favor you need:

PERSON ASKING FAVOR

1. ask for help
2. state problem
3. request favor
4. thank person for help

Use expressions like these:

Excuse me for . . .
I'm very sorry to bother you, but . . .
I hope you don't mind . . .
I (would) hate to have you/make you/
    ask you to . . .
I feel bad about . . .
I'm afraid that . . .
I was wondering if . . .
Would you mind . . .
Do you think you could . . .

PERSON DOING FAVOR

1. say you'll help
2. ask what you can do
3. say you'll do favor
4. tell person you don't mind

That's all right/That's OK.
Don't worry about it.
Don't mention it.
Forget it.
(It's) no problem/no trouble.

A. You have to take one of your children to the hospital.
You don't want to leave your other children alone.
Ask your neighbor to watch your children for you.

B. The motor on your refrigerator stopped working.
The repairman won't come until tomorrow.
You're afraid the food in your refrigerator will spoil.
Ask your neighbor for help.
You want to put your food in his refrigerator until yours is fixed.

C. You have bought a new rug for your living room at a discount store.
The store tied it on your car for you, and you brought it home.
Now you need help taking it into your house.
Ask your neighbor to help you.

D. You have to fill out your income tax return.
The form is very complicated, and you don't understand it.
You work with someone who is good with tax forms.
Ask this person to help you with your income tax form.

HAVE YOU FORGOTTEN ANYTHING?

LISTEN TO THESE PEOPLE.
They are talking about remembering and forgetting things.

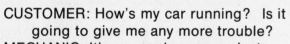

CUSTOMER: How's my car running? Is it going to give me any more trouble?

MECHANIC: It's as good as new. Just remember to take care of it from now on.

CUSTOMER: What do you mean?

MECHANIC: For one thing, make sure you change the oil and oil filter every 3,000 miles. Didn't you forget to do that the last time?

CUSTOMER: Yes, I guess I did forget about the oil filter.

MECHANIC: And don't forget to check the tires every now and then. Make sure they have the right pressure.

CUSTOMER: I'll try to remember. It's so easy to forget.

MECHANIC: While we're on the subject of forgetting things, aren't you forgetting something right now?

CUSTOMER: What?

MECHANIC: Haven't you forgotten about my bill?

CUSTOMER: Oh, I'm sorry. I almost forgot. Let me write you a check.

MECHANIC: You do have a terrible memory. Don't you remember? We don't accept personal checks.

CUSTOMER: Oh, all right. Here's my credit card.

MARY: Aren't you going to have the car checked out before we go away next week?

PETER: Yes. We'd better take it over to the gas station tomorrow. Let's make a list of what needs to be checked.

MARY: Well, don't forget to have them put in antifreeze. It's going to get pretty cold in the mountains. And remember to tell them to adjust the brakes. They haven't felt quite right lately.

PETER: Oh, and aren't we forgetting about the fan belt? I'd better have them change it.

MARY: And be sure to tell him to look at the spare tire. We don't want to get stuck with a flat spare.

PETER: Have we forgotten anything?

MARY: You may as well tell them to check the battery and the tire pressure while you're at it.

PETER: I'm sure glad we decided to make a list. I would never have remembered all this.

PRACTICE USING THESE WORDS.
Find them in the conversations on page 50.
Write what they mean. Write new sentences with them.

A. give someone trouble _____

_____

B. good as new _____

_____

C. from now on _____

_____

D. every now and then _____

_____

E. you may as well _____

_____

F. while you're at it _____

_____

TRY IT IN CLASS.
Practice with another student.

Use expressions like these:

Remember to . . .	Did you remember . . .	Aren't you going to . . .
Don't forget to . . .	Did you forget . . .	Didn't you forget . . .
Make sure you . . .	Have you remembered . . .	Haven't you forgotten . . .
Be sure to . . .	Have you forgotten . . .	Aren't you forgetting . . .

A. You are going on vacation. Your neighbor is going to take care of your house.
Remind your neighbor of the things that need to be done.
(1) bring in mail **(2)** water the lawn **(3)** water your plants **(4)** feed your dog

B. You are packing for a trip. You will be gone for a week.
Ask your husband/wife if he/she remembered to pack everything.
(1) toothbrush **(2)** first aid kit **(3)** the clothes you will need

C. You are a restaurant owner. You are training a new waiter.
Remind the new waiter of things he should do.
(1) ask if customer wants drink before taking order
(2) table number 4 hasn't been waited on; did waiter forget about them
(3) table number 3 has been finished eating for 15 minutes; isn't waiter
going to give them check
(4) waiter forgot to add tax on a check; remind him to add it

COMPLAINING AND EXPRESSING ANGER

LISTEN TO THESE PEOPLE.
One person is annoyed and is complaining.

CUSTOMER: Hello. This is John Peters. Is my car ready yet?

MECHANIC: I'm sorry Mr. Peters, your car isn't ready yet.

CUSTOMER: What? You've had it for over a week, and you still haven't fixed it.

MECHANIC: I'm sorry. We've been very busy lately.

CUSTOMER: Now wait just a minute. You promised the last time I called that it would be ready today.

MECHANIC: I don't know what else to say. It just isn't ready.

CUSTOMER: Look! I need my car. How much longer is this going to take?

MECHANIC: Who knows? It all depends on what's wrong with the car.

CUSTOMER: I beg your pardon. Do you mean to tell me that you haven't figured out what's wrong?

MECHANIC: Well, we think it's the generator.

CUSTOMER: You think? I don't believe this. Listen. I'm coming down tomorrow. If my car isn't ready, I'm going to have it towed at your expense to another garage.

MECHANIC: I'm sorry you feel that way. We do the best we can.

CUSTOMER: Well, it doesn't look like that's good enough.

CUSTOMER: Hello. This is Roberta Casals. I bought a car from you last week, and already I'm having trouble with it. The power steering went out yesterday. And today, it won't go into reverse!

SALESPERSON: That's too bad.

CUSTOMER: What? Is that all you're going to say? What are you going to do about it? I have a guarantee, you know.

SALESPERSON: Yes, I know. Why don't you have it towed to the lot? Our mechanic will take a look at it tomorrow.

CUSTOMER: I don't understand. Why can't you send a tow truck? And why can't your mechanic look at it today?

SALESPERSON: Our mechanic is all booked up for today. He won't be able to get to your car until tomorrow. And I'm afraid towing is not our responsibility.

CUSTOMER: All right. But tell me this. When will I get my car back?

SALESPERSON: Probably not until next week. Repairs like these take time.

CUSTOMER: Next week! But I need my car for work. I can't do without it. Can't you do any better than that?

SALESPERSON: What can I tell you? It's the best we can do.

CUSTOMER: Really? After you make the sale, you don't care what happens, do you? You can be sure that I won't recommend you to any of my friends.

PRACTICE USING THESE WORDS.
Find them in the conversations on page 52.
Write what they mean.   Write new sentences with them.

A. it all depends on _____

_____

B. to figure out _____

_____

C. do something about it _____

_____

D. be booked up _____

_____

E. can't do without _____

_____

TALK TOPICS

A.   Do you think the customers on page 52 should be angry?
B.   Would you say what these customers said?
        How would you have handled the problems?

WHAT DO YOU SAY?
Practice with another student.   Choose what you will say, line A or line B.
Only one line is the correct thing to say.

	CUSTOMER	CLERK
1.	**A.** I'm here to pick up my watch. **B.** I want my watch please.	**A.** So what. It isn't ready. **B.** I'm sorry. It isn't ready.
2.	**A.** But you promised it would be ready today. **B.** But I want it today.	**A.** What can I say? We haven't been able to fix it yet. **B.** I'm afraid that's not our responsibility.
3.	**A.** Look. I need my watch. When will it be ready? **B.** Wait just a minute. You've got to fix that watch.	**A.** Who knows? It isn't ready today. **B.** It all depends on what's wrong with it.
4.	**A.** What are you going to do about it? I need my watch. **B.** Listen. Just give me my watch. I'll take it someplace else.	**A.** I'm sorry you feel that way. We do the best we can. **B.** That's too bad. I'm really sorry.

TRY IT IN CLASS.
Practice with another student.

Use expressions like these:

PERSON COMPLAINING	PERSON RESPONDING
Look/Now look here.	That's too bad.
Listen.	What can I tell you?
Now (wait) just a minute.	I don't know what (else) to say.
I beg your pardon.	I'm sorry you feel that way.
Can't you/Why can't you . . .	Who knows?
You promised/were supposed to . . .	It all depends on . . .

A. The customer is returning an alarm radio. The alarm doesn't work.

CUSTOMER	CLERK
1. state your problem	1. you can't help; customer should leave it for your repairman
2. you want new radio; don't want to have this one repaired	2. you don't have any more radios like this one
3. you need alarm to get you up for work	3. you understand but you can't do anything more about it
4. you want refund; you'll buy a new alarm radio at another store	4. can't give refund; all sales are final
5. you will leave radio for repairs, but you are not happy about it	5. apologize and promise to have radio repaired as soon as possible

B. The customer is picking up a suit at the dry cleaners.

CUSTOMER	CLERK
1. you want to pick up your suit	1. give customer the suit
2. you find a stain on it	2. not your fault; already stained
3. no stain on it when you brought it in; cleaners ruined your suit	3. not possible; customer must be mistaken
4. you need suit for important interview; store must remove stain	4. customer should leave suit
5. need it tomorrow	5. not possible; will take three days
6. sign in window says same-day service	6. not on suits
7. you'll take suit as is and clean it yourself; you won't use cleaners again	7. apologize

C. You've been waiting for an hour for a cab. You're now late for work. Call cab company and complain.

D. You stayed home from work to wait for telephone company to install a phone. It is now 3:00 in the afternoon and no one has showed up. Call to complain.

E. You ordered dinner a half hour ago. You still haven't been served. Complain to the waiter.

CLOSE-UP ON LANGUAGE

These four tenses can be used to talk about the past:

the past tense	He <u>lived</u> here in 1972.
the past continuous tense	He <u>was living</u> here when I moved in.
the past perfect tense	He <u>had lived</u> here before I moved in.
the past perfect continuous tense	He <u>had been living</u> there while we were away.

THE PAST TENSE

You can use the past tense in the following types of sentences:

We <u>played</u> baseball on Sundays.	I <u>ate</u> fresh vegetables all summer.
Bob <u>was</u> a happy child.	They <u>seemed</u> upset.
Jefferson <u>was born</u> in 1743.	They <u>took</u> the 8 o'clock train.

The past tense of regular verbs is formed by adding <u>-ed</u>.
You will need to memorize forms of irregular verbs.

FILL IN THE MISSING WORDS.
Use the past tense of the verb in parentheses.

A. Mary _____talked_____ to Bill yesterday.   (to talk)

B. Tom _____ a mechanic in the Air Force.   (to be)

C. We _____ the driving test.   (to pass)

D. I _____ to school when I was a child.   (to walk)

E. She _____ her gray dress to the wedding.   (to wear)

F. They _____ this house in 1975.   (to buy)

G. The TV _____ always on at dinnertime.   (to be)

H. He _____ this picture when he was in Paris.   (to take)

I. I _____ that book three times.   (to read)

J. My husband _____ you an hour ago.   (to call)

K. The movie _____ very interesting.   (to be)

L. Every afternoon, we _____ to the library to study.   (to go)

M. On holidays, we _____ a lamb.   (to cook)

N. I _____ you at the park last Sunday.   (to see)

O. The sky _____ beautiful at sunset today.   (to be)

THE PAST CONTINUOUS TENSE

Notice how the past continuous tense is used:

> I was sleeping when the phone rang.
> We were watching TV last night.

This tense is formed with the past tense of be (was/were) + verb + -ing.

FILL IN THE MISSING WORDS.
Use the past continuous tense of the verb in parentheses.

A. It _____was snowing_____ when we left work yesterday. (to snow)

B. The phone _____ when I got home. (to ring)

C. We _____ before you came in. (to talk)

D. They _____ me about the neighborhood. (to ask)

E. The sun _____ yesterday. (to shine)

F. I _____ about you last night. (to dream)

G. I _____ in line for hours. (to wait)

H. We _____ at their house while they were away. (to stay)

I. They _____ over there a minute ago. (to sit)

J. You _____ as a waitress before, weren't you? (to work)

K. He _____ along with that record. (to sing)

L. They _____ for you. (to look)

M. I _____ Rita last week. (to visit)

N. We _____ in the checkout line when the store closed. (to stand)

O. I _____ to her sales pitch, but I didn't believe her. (to listen)

THE PAST PERFECT TENSE

Notice how the past perfect tense is used:

> He told me that the fire had burned everything.
> They had left before we arrived.

This tense is formed with had + the past participle.

COMBINE THESE SENTENCES.
Use the past perfect tense. Use <u>before</u> to connect the sentences.

A. We talked for hours. We went out for dinner.

      We had talked for hours before we went out for dinner.

B. I looked at many cars. I bought this one.

_____

C. She finished her dinner. The waiter brought the wine.

_____

D. We knew each other for 10 years. We got married.

_____

E. He bought the truck. He noticed that the brakes were bad.

_____

F. Kim studied the driver's manual. She took the driving test.

_____

G. I left the restaurant. I realized my wallet was missing.

_____

H. Anna looked for another job. She quit her job at the store.

_____

I. He finished his work. He went on vacation.

_____

J. Everyone went home. I left the office.

_____

THE PAST PERFECT CONTINUOUS TENSE

You can use the past perfect continuous tense in the following types of sentences:

She <u>had been waiting</u> more than an hour for us.
They <u>had been driving</u> everywhere until gas became so expensive.

Notice that this tense is formed with <u>had</u> + <u>been</u> + verb + <u>-ing</u>.

FILL IN THE MISSING WORDS.
Use the past perfect continuous tense of the verb in parentheses.

A. They ____had been waiting____ outside for ten minutes before he opened the

   door.   (to wait)

B. He _____ for 9 hours before we woke him up.   (to sleep)

C. I _____ before I moved here.   (to travel)

D. We _____ a long time when we finally found a gas

   station.   (to drive)

E. You _____ about inviting her, hadn't you?   (to think)

F. They _____ about me when I walked in.   (to talk)

G. She _____ TV when the lights went out.   (to watch)

H. I _____ that book until Carmen took it.   (to read)

I. We _____ the car when the rain started.   (to fix)

J. They _____ secretly on Thursdays.   (to meet)

NEGATIVES

Past Tense	We saw her yesterday.	We <u>did not</u> (<u>didn't</u>) <u>see</u> her yesterday.
	He called me today.	He <u>didn't</u> <u>call</u> me today.
	I was late.	I <u>was not</u> (<u>wasn't</u>) late.
	They were ready.	They <u>were not</u> (<u>weren't</u>) ready.
Past Continuous Tense	They were listening to you.	They <u>weren't listening</u> to you.
	He was working.	He <u>wasn't working</u>.
Past Perfect Tense	I had driven that car before.	I <u>had not</u> (<u>hadn't</u>) <u>driven</u> that car before.
Past Perfect Continuous Tense	He <u>had been talking</u> in class.	He <u>hadn't been talking</u> in class.

REWRITE THESE SENTENCES.
Use the negative.

A. They <u>spoke</u> to me about it last week.

   _____They didn't speak to me about it last week._____

B. I <u>had learned</u> how to drive before I bought a car.

   _____

C. She <u>was talking</u> to you.

_____

D. The car <u>had been giving</u> us a lot of trouble before we sold it.

_____

E. Her clothes <u>were</u> very expensive.

_____

F. It <u>was raining</u> when I left the house.

_____

G. We <u>went</u> out to eat last night.

_____

H. Their coats <u>were hanging</u> in the closet.

_____

I. The tire <u>had been</u> flat when I bought it.

_____

J. She <u>had been talking</u> about you before you came in.

_____

QUESTIONS

Past Tense

<u>Did</u> you <u>find</u> your glasses?
<u>Was</u> he surprised to see you?
<u>Were</u> they at home when you arrived?

Past Continuous Tense

Was the sun <u>shining</u> this morning?
<u>Were</u> you <u>talking</u> to me?

Past Perfect Tense

<u>Had</u> you <u>been</u> there before?

Past Perfect Continuous Tense

<u>Had</u> they <u>been dating</u> each other for a long time?

WRITE QUESTIONS.

A. <u>Were you sleeping when I called</u> ? No, I wasn't sleeping when you called.

B. _____ ? Yes, they had been singing earlier.

C. _____ ? No, I didn't drive past your house yesterday.

D. _____ ? Yes, they had written to each other before.

E. _____ ? No, we weren't eating when you called.

F. _____ ? Yes, the heat had been on all last winter.

G. _____ ? No, I didn't lock the door.

H. _____ ? Yes, she had been playing the piano.

I. _____ ? No, he didn't build this house by himself.

J. _____ ? Yes, you were talking in your sleep.

K. _____ ? No, we hadn't been out last night.

L. _____ ? Yes, we had looked under the bed.

M. _____ ? No, he didn't answer the phone.

N. _____ ? Yes, she was working this morning.

O. _____ ? No, they hadn't been staying here.

P. _____ ? Yes, they had left the door open.

NEGATIVE QUESTIONS

Past Tense

Didn't you lose your sweater?
Wasn't he helpful?
Weren't they ready to buy?

Past Continuous Tense

Wasn't she working in that restaurant?
Weren't they giving away toasters at Carson's?

Past Perfect Tense

Hadn't he cleaned before you arrived?

Past Perfect Continuous Tense

Hadn't they been planning a vacation?

WRITE QUESTIONS.
Use the negative.

A. _____Didn't he walk to work_____ ? Yes, he walked to work.

B. _____ ? No, she wasn't helping us.

C. _____ ? Yes, I had been away during the storm.

D. _____ ? No, I hadn't been watching TV earlier.

E. _____ ? Yes, they were kind to us.

F. _____ ? No, I hadn't been waiting a long time.

G. _____ ? Yes, he was typing a letter.

60

TALKING ABOUT THE FUTURE

There are four ways of talking about the future:

will + verb	They will (they'll) be here at 8 o'clock.
be + going to + verb	I am going to buy a new car soon.
the present tense	The movie begins at 7:30.
the present continuous tense	We are taking our vacation next month.

FILL IN THE MISSING WORDS.
Talk about the future.   Use will + verb or be + going to + verb.

A. I _____ am going to start _____ a diet next week.   (to start)

B. The movie _____ over at 9:30.   (to be)

C. They _____ the present you bought them.   (to like)

D. That chair _____ nice in your living room.   (to look)

E. I _____ you after class.   (to meet)

F. He _____ in on May 30th.   (to move)

G. We _____ it over.   (to think)

H. You _____ how well this car handles.   (to love)

I. I _____ you tomorrow at noon.   (to call)

J. You _____ your car this afternoon.   (to have)

LOOK AT THESE SENTENCES.
Put a 1 in the box if the sentence is about the future.
Put a 2 in the box if the sentence is about the present.

A. ☐ We are taking the 10 o'clock train tonight.

B. ☐ She is wearing a long dress to the party next week.

C. ☐ School ends tomorrow.

D. ☐ He is standing near the window.

E. ☐ The race starts at 1:30.

F. ☐ I'm getting tired of all the mistakes they make.

G. ☐ He gets out of work at 5 o'clock this evening.

H. ☐ Your mother is waiting for you at the bus stop.

I. ☐ They're coming for a visit in a few weeks.

J. ☐ His sister plays a violin in the orchestra.

NEGATIVES

<u>will</u> + verb	He <u>will not</u> (won't) be home on time. They <u>will not</u> (won't) <u>come</u> back.
<u>be</u> + <u>going to</u> + verb	He <u>is not</u> (isn't) <u>going to play</u> ball today. I <u>am</u> (I'm) <u>not going to make</u> dinner tonight. We <u>are not</u> (aren't) <u>going to buy</u> any food at this store.

REWRITE THESE SENTENCES.
Make these negative.   Use contractions.

A. We are going to have a picnic this weekend.

<u>   We aren't going to have a picnic this weekend.   </u>

B. They will take a long vacation this year.

_____

C. It's going to be a very warm day tomorrow.

_____

D. You will be very surprised when you see what's in the package.

_____

E. She's going to learn how to drive.

_____

F. He will move out at the end of the month.

_____

G. I'll be back in time for dinner.

_____

H. You're going to like the food at that restaurant.

_____

I. You'll find another car that you like as much as this one.

_____

J. Today is going to be a good day.

_____

K. We'll see each other again in the fall.

_____

L. They are going to drive home tonight.

_____

QUESTIONS

will + verb   Will he be here on time?
                            Will you help me?

be + going to + verb   Is she going to get her driver's license?
                            Am I going to pass the test?
                            Are you going to talk to George?

WRITE QUESTIONS.

A.   Are you going to the park today   ?   Yes, I'm going to the park today.

B. _____ ?   No, I won't see you later.

C. _____ ?   Yes, he is going to answer your questions.

D. _____ ?   No, that letter isn't going to arrive today.

E. _____ ?   Yes, this car will get good gas mileage.

F. _____ ?   No, the mechanic won't fix it tomorrow.

G. _____ ?   Yes, I'm going to finish on time.

H. _____ ?   No, we won't be there on Tuesday.

I. _____ ?   Yes, they'll be ready soon.

J. _____ ?   No, it's not going to rain.

NEGATIVE QUESTIONS

will + verb   Won't he be here on time?
                            Won't you stay for dinner?

be + going to + verb   Isn't she going to come with us?
                            Aren't you going to eat anything?

WRITE QUESTIONS.

A.   Won't I get to work faster by train   ?   Yes, you'll get to work faster by train.

B. _____ ?   No, I'm not going to apply for that job.

C. _____ ?   Yes, we'll call you later.

D. _____ ?   No, they're not going to be helpful.

E. _____ ?   Yes, she'll be back again.

F. _____ ?   No, I'm not going to talk about you.

G. _____ ?   Yes, he'll sell you a good used car.

H. _____ ?   No, they won't believe you.

UNIT 3

KEEP UP THE GOOD WORK

IN THIS UNIT, YOU WILL BE:

giving and responding to praise, criticism, and warnings

asking your boss for an opinion about your work

making and thinking about suggestions

giving and following directions

asking for help from someone you know

asking for and giving permission

talking about what someone has to do

In the Close-Up on Language, you will review:

the past tense and the past participles of irregular verbs

pronouns (subject, object, possessive, reflexive, and indefinite)

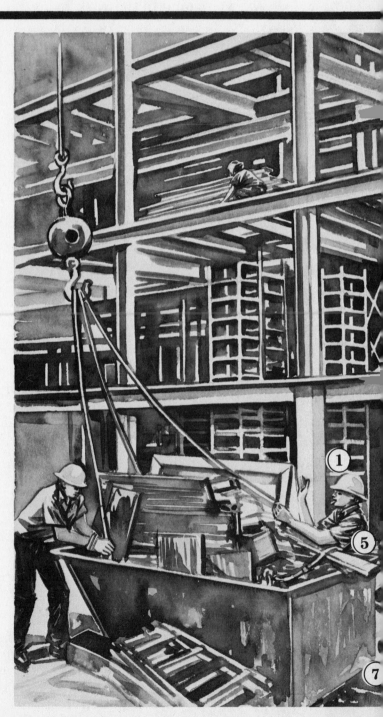

LOOK AT THE PICTURE.
Find these things in the picture.

1. hard hat
2. goggles/safety glasses
3. construction worker
4. lumber
5. bricks
6. trailer
7. shovel
8. bucket/pail
9. wheelbarrow
10. truck

TALK TOPICS

LOOK AT THE PICTURE.
Talk about what you see.

What is this place?
What are these people doing?

Name some of the jobs that these people
    have. What are their job duties?
Do you have a job? If so, what do you do?

What are the workers wearing for
    safety? Why should the workers
    wear these things?

Many workers in the United States belong
    to unions. Are there labor unions in
    your native country? If so, are they
    different from U.S. labor unions?

Pretend to be one of the people in the
    picture. What were you doing in the
    picture on page 65? What are you
    doing now? What are you saying?

ASK QUESTIONS ABOUT THE PICTURE.
Write down the new words and expressions you want to remember.

11. _____   16. _____
12. _____   17. _____
13. _____   18. _____
14. _____   19. _____
15. _____   20. _____

OFFERING PRAISE AND ADVICE

LISTEN TO THESE PEOPLE.
Mr. Falvo likes the job Lan is doing.   He wants to give Lan a new job.

MR. FALVO: Lan, I want to have a word with you. I'm very pleased with your work. You're a very hard worker. We need employees like you.

LAN: Thank you, Mr. Falvo. I enjoy working here.

MR. FALVO: Glad to hear it. You know, I think you're ready to move on now. I need another cashier for the store. I think you should apply for the job.

LAN: I don't know what to say, Mr. Falvo. Thanks for asking me. I'm just not sure that I could handle the job.

MR. FALVO: Oh, you'd catch on quickly. And of course someone would train you. Don't sell yourself short. Think it over.

LAN: OK. I'll think about it this weekend. Thanks for the offer.

MR. FALVO: Keep up the good work.

PRACTICE USING THESE WORDS.
Find them in the conversation.
Write what they mean.   Write new sentences with them.

A.   to have a word with (someone) _____

_____

B.   to move on _____

_____

C.   to handle the job _____

_____

D.   to catch on _____

_____

E.   to sell (someone) short _____

_____

TRY IT IN CLASS.
Practice with another student.
A boss is praising an employee and giving the employee some advice.

Use expressions like these:

BOSS		EMPLOYEE
I'm pleased with your work.	If I were you . . .	I'm glad you think . . .
You're doing a good job.	Take my advice . . .	Thanks for . . .
Keep up the good work.	I think you should . . .	I'm just not sure . . .
You catch on fast.	The best thing for you . . .	I'll think it over . . .

A. A bus driver is talking about a new job with the boss.

BOSS	EMPLOYEE
1. you like employee's work; say so	1. thank your boss
2. you think driver should apply for job as manager	2. you don't like the idea—you like working with the public, and you don't like paperwork
3. you think driver is wrong; manager's job would give raise and better hours	3. agree to think about it

B. A secretary is talking to the boss about learning a new job.

BOSS	EMPLOYEE
1. you like secretary's work; say so	1. thank your boss
2. you think secretary should learn how to use computer	2. you don't like the idea—it looks too hard to learn
3. say you'll pay for any training; you think secretary learns quickly	3. agree to try

C. A factory worker is talking to the boss about a job.

BOSS	EMPLOYEE
1. you like employee's work; say so	1. thank your boss; you like your job but you need more money
2. you can't give employee raise; you think employee should work night shift—more money	2. you don't like the idea—you would be away from family too much; you'll think it over

D. The boss of a warehouse likes an employee's work. The boss tells the employee. The boss also says that the employee should become a driver for the company. The employee doesn't know how to drive a truck.

PLEASE TRY HARDER

LISTEN TO THESE PEOPLE.
They are talking about problems with the employee's work.

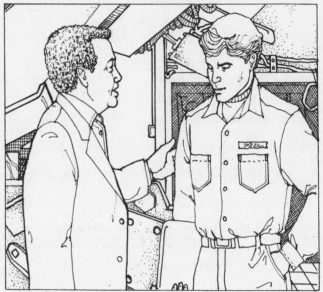

MS. BROWN: Rita, I want to have a word with you. It's about your work.

RITA: Yes, Ms. Brown?

MS. BROWN: I asked you to have this letter ready yesterday. You're running behind schedule and slowing things down.

RITA: I'm sorry that I was late, but people are always calling me. I never have enough time to work.

MS. BROWN: I think you should talk to your friends after work, Rita. If you don't try harder, you'll find yourself out of work.

RITA: I'll try my best, Ms. Brown.

MS. BROWN: Please do. I don't want to fire you.

GEORGE: I'd like to talk to you, Mike.

MIKE: Sure, George.

GEORGE: I've noticed that you haven't been doing your share of the work. And you aren't getting along very well with everybody. Now, I don't want to lose a good worker. So tell me what's wrong.

MIKE: I'm not really sure. I've been feeling very tired lately. I can't get to sleep at night. Everything upsets me.

GEORGE: When was your last vacation?

MIKE: Let's see. It's been over a year.

GEORGE: Maybe you need a break, Mike. If I were you, I'd go soon.

PRACTICE USING THESE WORDS.
Find them in the conversations.
Write what they mean. Write new sentences with them.

A. to have (something) ready _____

_____

B. to run behind schedule _____

_____

C. to slow (something) down _____

_____

D. to have time _____

_____

E. to find yourself out of work _____

_____

F. to try your best _____

_____

G. to get along with (someone) _____

_____

H. let's see _____

_____

I. to need a break _____

_____

TALK TOPICS
Look at the conversations on pages 68 and 70. Answer these questions in class.

A. What did Mr. Falvo say Lan should do? Why didn't Lan accept the job immediately? Did Lan have a good reason? What would you do if you were Lan?

B. What was the problem with Rita's work? What was the problem with Mike's work? Were Rita's excuses good? Were Mike's excuses good? What warning did each boss give? What would you say to Rita? What would you say to Mike?

C. Notice what Lan, Rita, and Mike call their employers. Notice what their employers call them. Do you call your boss by his/her first name? What do you like to be called?

D. Read the following sentences. You are the boss. What would you say to the employee?

1. A factory worker uses dangerous machines. She also works another job at night. She isn't always careful because she is too tired.

2. A receptionist is often rude to callers and visitors. He says that he is too busy to be polite to people.

3. A salesperson gets to work late and goes home early every day. Even though the salesperson works fewer hours than the other salespeople, she sells more.

AM I DOING THIS RIGHT?

LISTEN TO THESE PEOPLE.
The employee is asking the boss about his/her work.
The boss is talking about the employee's work.

ROBERTO: Am I doing this right, Ms. Luck?

MS. LUCK: Let's see. Yes, Roberto. That's just fine—perfect.

ROBERTO: Good. I want to do this correctly. I know it's important not to make mistakes.

MS. LUCK: That's true, Roberto. It is important. And you're learning very quickly.

ROBERTO: It's nice of you to say that.

BOB: Is this the way you wanted the report typed, Carmen?

CARMEN: No, it's not. This isn't at all what I had in mind. Didn't you listen to me when I explained it?

BOB: Yes, I did listen to you. I thought this was what you wanted.

CARMEN: I'm afraid not. Well, I don't want to waste any more time. Don't retype it. But please be more careful next time.

BETTY: Have I been working quickly enough, Mr. Long?

MR. LONG: Well, no, Betty. You've been rather slow. Your line is always the longest one in the store. What's the trouble?

BETTY: I'm still learning how to use the cash register. I'm sorry to cause a problem.

MR. LONG: I know you're trying, Betty. Perhaps you should work a shift when there aren't so many customers. In the meantime, do the best you can.

Practice with another student.
An employee is talking to the boss about his/her work.

Use expressions like these:

EMPLOYEE	BOSS	
Am I doing . . . right?	That's fine/good/perfect.	What's the trouble?
Are you happy with my work?	I'm pleased with . . .	I'm not happy with . . .
Have I been working . . . enough?	You're doing a good job.	If you don't . . .
Is this . . . the way you wanted?		I'm afraid that . . .

A. An employee in a bakery is showing the boss a special cake that he/she made.

EMPLOYEE	BOSS
1. ask if boss likes the cake	**1.** you like the cake—it's beautiful
2. thank boss	**2.** thank employee; more people will come to bakery to buy his/her cakes

B. A mechanic in a repair shop is talking to the boss.

EMPLOYEE	BOSS
1. ask boss if you fixed car correctly	**1.** no—part missing
2. you'll try again	**2.** no—you will fix car; mechanic should watch and help
3. thank boss for checking car; apologize for your mistake	

C. The manager of a fruit and vegetable stand is talking to the owner.

EMPLOYEE	BOSS
1. ask if you are selling enough produce (fruits & vegetables)	**1.** you think employee is doing a great job—stand sells more produce than other stands
2. thank boss	**2.** say you'll give employee a bigger store to manage
3. you don't like the idea—you like the store you have	**3.** employee could have better hours and higher salary
4. agree to think about it	**4.** you think employee should accept new store

D. A gardener cuts all the bushes around the owner's house. The owner doesn't like the way it looks.

MAKING SUGGESTIONS

LISTEN TO THESE PEOPLE.
One person is making suggestions.
The other person is responding to the suggestions.

MR. DALE: How's your work going, Mark?

MARK: Fine, Mr. Dale. I've been putting away these office supplies. I'm almost done.

MR. DALE: You know, Mark, it might be a good idea to redo these shelves. It would be better if the pens and paper were on the middle shelf. They should be easy to reach. Then you ought to put the old files on the top shelf. And why don't you put those big boxes on the bottom shelf?

MARK: I think you're right, Mr. Dale. I'll try it your way.

MARY: Anna, can I talk to you about something?

ANNA: Sure, Mary. What is it?

MARY: I have a suggestion. Have you thought about having two people work together on one project?

ANNA: Well, I don't know. What makes you think that would work better?

MARY: It seems to me that partners would keep each other going. They could give each other suggestions and share ideas.

ANNA: Yes, but they might not get as much work done if they're always talking to each other.

MARY: Perhaps we could try it. You could give it a couple of months and see if it works.

ANNA: That's a good suggestion. I'll agree to a two-month trial period. We'll see how it goes.

MARY: That's great, Anna. Thank you.

ANNA: Thanks for making the suggestion, Mary.

PRACTICE USING THESE WORDS.
Find them in the conversations.
Write what they mean. Write new sentences with them.

A. how's . . . going _____

_____

B. to put (something) away _____

_____

C. to be done _____

_____

D. what makes you think that . . . _____

_____

E. keep (someone/something) going _____

_____

F. to give (someone/something) some time _____

_____

G. to see how it goes _____

_____

WHAT DO YOU SAY?
Choose what you will say, line A or line B.
Only one line is the correct thing to say.

	WAITER	MANAGER
1.	**A.** Could I talk to you about my work hours? **B.** I don't like the hours you told me to work this week.	**A.** Oh, that's too bad. **B.** Of course. Is there a problem?
2.	**A.** I'm not working in the morning and at night. I'll be too tired. **B.** You'd like me to work in the morning and at night. I think that might be hard for me. I'd be working late and getting up early.	**A.** You may be right. What do you suggest we do? **B.** What do you want me to do about it?
3.	**A.** I think it would be better if I worked in the morning and in the afternoon. Perhaps another waiter would like to work at night. **B.** I want to work in the morning and in the afternoon. Make somebody else work at night.	**A.** I don't think I can find someone else to work at night. I'm afraid you'll have to work. **B.** I'm not making any changes.

TRY IT IN CLASS.
Practice with another student.

Use expressions like these:

PERSON MAKING SUGGESTION

I have a suggestion.
It might be a good idea to . . .
It seems to me that . . .
Perhaps we could . . .
It would be better . . .
I think you ought/should . . .

What do you think about . . . ?
Have you thought about . . . ?
Why don't you . . . ?
Why not . . . ?
How/what about . . . ?

PERSON RESPONDING TO SUGGESTION

That's a good idea/suggestion . . .
Sounds like a good idea . . .
That's a good suggestion . . .
I'll agree with that.
You may be right . . .
I'll give it a try.
We'll see how . . .

What makes you think . . . ?
Well, I don't know . . .
Yes, but . . .
It might be better, but . . .

A. An office manager is complaining that the clerks take too much time for lunch.

OFFICE MANAGER	CLERK
1. employees spend too much time out of office at lunchtime	1. explain that service in nearby coffee shop is slow—lunch takes too long
2. ask employees how they can shorten time away from work	2. suggest making a lunchroom in office—need tables, chairs, and refrigerator
3. agree; thank clerk for suggestion	3. thank manager for listening

B. A cook is talking to the manager.

COOK	MANAGER
1. you're too busy to do a good job; you think manager should hire a kitchen helper	1. you don't have enough money to hire a kitchen helper
2. suggest that manager let fewer customers in restaurant—then you wouldn't be as busy	2. you can't do that—you'd lose money; you think cook should make food in morning—then warm it for customers
3. you don't like the idea—food wouldn't taste good; suggest that manager help in kitchen	3. you can't help in kitchen—you're too busy
4. again suggest that manager hire a kitchen helper	4. agree to try out a helper

76

FOLLOWING DIRECTIONS

LISTEN TO THESE PEOPLE.
Mrs. Herbert is giving directions to her assistant, Tony.

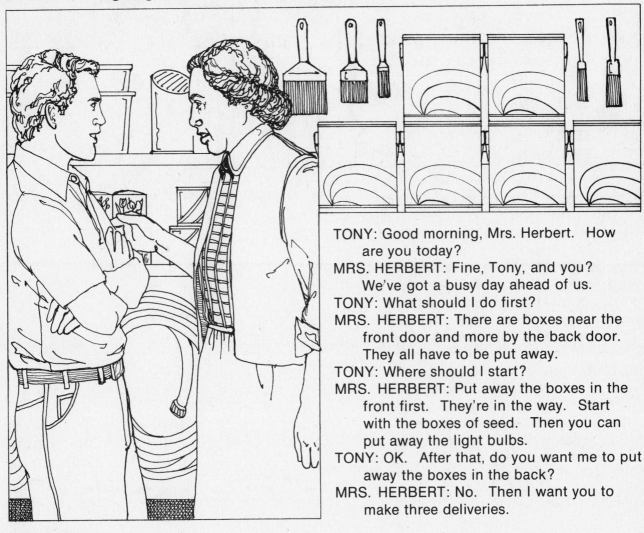

TONY: Good morning, Mrs. Herbert. How are you today?

MRS. HERBERT: Fine, Tony, and you? We've got a busy day ahead of us.

TONY: What should I do first?

MRS. HERBERT: There are boxes near the front door and more by the back door. They all have to be put away.

TONY: Where should I start?

MRS. HERBERT: Put away the boxes in the front first. They're in the way. Start with the boxes of seed. Then you can put away the light bulbs.

TONY: OK. After that, do you want me to put away the boxes in the back?

MRS. HERBERT: No. Then I want you to make three deliveries.

TALK TOPICS
Read the conversation.
Answer these questions.

A. What should Tony do first, make the deliveries or put away the light bulbs?

B. Which boxes have to be put away first—the ones in the front or the ones in the back?

C. How many deliveries does Tony have to make?

D. Should Tony put away the boxes in the back before he makes the deliveries?

E. List what Tony has to do. Put the list in the order that Mrs. Herbert gave.

F. Pretend you are Tony's boss. Tell him what you want him to do. Don't use the order that Mrs. Herbert gave.

LISTEN TO THESE PEOPLE.
Mrs. Herbert is giving more directions to Tony.

TONY: What should I do this afternoon? Didn't you want me to straighten out the nails and screws? That's what you told me yesterday.

MRS. HERBERT: I don't know whether you'll have time for that. We'll see how the day goes. I've got to go out this afternoon. I'll need you to answer the phone and wait on the customers.

TONY: Will you be back by closing time?

MRS. HERBERT: I don't think so. I'm leaving at three. You can close the store. Don't forget to count the money and fill out a bank deposit slip.

TONY: Should I deposit the money on my way home?

MRS. HERBERT: Would you mind?

TONY: Of course not. I'd be glad to.

TALK TOPICS
Read the conversation.
Answer these questions.

A. What should Tony do first, wait on the customers or go to the bank?

B. Which job comes first—counting the money or filling out a bank deposit slip?

C. When should Tony deposit the money?

D. Who will wait on the customers at 4:00?

E. List what Tony has to do. Put the list in the order that Mrs. Herbert gave.

F. Pretend that you are Tony's boss. Tell him to put the money in the store safe instead of the bank.

78

PRACTICE USING THESE WORDS.
Find them in the conversations on pages 77 and 78.
Write what they mean.   Write new sentences with them.

A. to have a busy day ahead _____

_____

B. to be in the way _____

_____

C. to make a delivery _____

_____

D. to have time _____

_____

E. to see how the day goes _____

_____

F. to wait on (someone) _____

_____

G. on (someone's) way _____

_____

H. to mind doing (something) _____

_____

TRY IT IN CLASS.
Practice with another student.
One student gives a set of directions and the other student follows them.
Give one step at a time.

Set A	Set B
1. Close book.	1. Take out piece of paper.
2. Pick up pen/pencil.	2. Print name in upper right-hand corner.
3. Put pen/pencil in front of book.	3. Write address under name.
4. Take out piece of paper.	4. Print date in upper left-hand corner.
5. Write last name in top left corner.	5. Write date of birth in bottom left-hand corner.
6. Fold paper in half.	6. Draw circle in middle of paper.
7. Open book to page 60.	7. Make circle into clock face—number from 1 to 12 around circle.
8. Write first word of page 60 on bottom of folded paper.	8. Show what time it is now.
9. Put paper in book.	
10. Give book to me.	

COULD YOU HELP ME?

LISTEN TO THESE PEOPLE.
These coworkers are helping each other.

LEE: Would you mind showing me how to change this typewriter ribbon?

CARLA: To tell the truth, I'm not so sure myself. I always get Toby to do it for me.

LEE: He's out sick today. Do you know anyone else who can help me? I've got to finish typing this letter.

CARLA: Let's try it ourselves. There are directions on the box. I'm sure we can figure out what to do.

LEE: OK. I appreciate your help.

CARLA: Sure. It's no trouble.

YOKO: Rick, what should I do when a customer gets angry? Do you know how to calm him down?

RICK: To be honest with you, I can't always calm a really angry customer. But it is good to try. Always be polite. Offer the customer a seat. Find out what's wrong. Then try to straighten out the problem quickly. Apologize if the store made a mistake.

YOKO: Thanks a lot, Rick. You've been very helpful.

RICK: You're welcome. Glad to help.

TERESA: Could you tell me how to make a "Super Sundae"? I've never made one before.

SARAH: I'd be glad to. Get a big sundae dish.

TERESA: Like this one?

SARAH: Right. Fill it with five scoops of vanilla ice cream.

TERESA: OK. Now what?

SARAH: Pour strawberry, chocolate, and butterscotch topping over the ice cream. Then add whipped cream and nuts.

TERESA: That's easy enough. Thanks for telling me what to do.

SARAH: Not at all.

PRACTICE USING THESE WORDS.
Find them in the conversations on page 80.
Write what they mean. Write new sentences with them.

A.   to get (someone) to do (something) _____

_____

B.   to be out sick _____

_____

C.   to figure out what to do _____

_____

D.   be honest with _____

_____

E.   that's easy enough _____

_____

F.   not at all _____

_____

WHAT DO YOU SAY?
Choose what you will say, line A or line B.
Only one line is the correct thing to say.

	CLERK	LIBRARIAN
1.	A. Excuse me, could you please help me? B. Help me, please.	A. Certainly. B. What do you want?
2.	A. The book that I'm supposed to find isn't on the shelf. Do you know where it could be? B. I'm looking for a book. You'll tell me where to find it.	A. Maybe. B. Someone may have borrowed it. Did you look for it in Bob's office?
3.	A. Would you mind? B. Yes, I did. It wasn't there. Where else should I look?	A. Look in Marta's office. It may be there. B. Not at all. It's around here somewhere.
4.	A. Thank you. I'll look there. It's very nice of you to help me. B. That doesn't help me.	A. That's too bad. B. It's no problem.

Use expressions like these:

ASKING FOR HELP		GIVING HELP
Would you mind . . . ?	I appreciate your help.	It's no trouble.
Do you know . . . ?	Thanks a lot.	Not at all.
Could you . . . ?	It's nice of you to	You're welcome.
How do I . . . ?	You've been very helpful.	It's quite all right.
Is this right?		Glad to help.

A. A new employee at a gas station is asking a coworker about the job.

NEW EMPLOYEE	COWORKER
1. ask coworker to tell you what to do while you're filling a car with gas	1. tell coworker to wash car windows
2. ask what to do next	2. tell coworker to check oil and water
3. ask what to do next	3. tell coworker to ask if customer is paying with cash or charge
4. thank coworker for help	4. accept thanks

B. A new employee is asking a coworker how to use the office telephone.

NEW EMPLOYEE	COWORKER
1. ask coworker for help	1. agree to help coworker; give coworker the office telephone directory
2. ask how to call people who don't work in office	2. tell coworker to dial "9" and the number
3. thank coworker	3. accept thanks

C. A sales clerk in a shoe store is asking a coworker to help find a box of shoes.

SALES CLERK	COWORKER
1. ask coworker to help you find a pair of size 7 brown shoes	1. ask if coworker has looked on top shelf
2. yes; ask if coworker can think of another place to look	2. could be on bottom shelf
3. you checked bottom shelf	3. the shoes might have been sold
4. thank coworker	4. accept thanks

D. Two waiters are talking. One is asking what to do when a customer doesn't like the food.

CAN I? . . . CAN'T I?

LISTEN TO THESE PEOPLE.
They are talking about what they are allowed to do (permission)
and what they must do (obligation).

MARY: Excuse me, Mr. Wong. I'd like to know if it's all right to take Friday off.
MR. WONG: You know Friday is our busiest day.
MARY: Yes, I do. But I have to see the doctor, and she's only free on Friday.
MR. WONG: In that case, of course you can take the day off.

KIM: Barbara, are we allowed to take cigarette breaks?
BARBARA: Yes, as long as you don't take too many.
KIM: Can I go anytime I want or do I have to tell someone?
BARBARA: Just make sure that someone's watching your tables while you're gone.
KIM: All right. Thanks.

FRED: Pete, I've noticed that you haven't been wearing your hard hat.
PETE: Isn't it all right to go without it? I don't like the way it feels.
FRED: No, it isn't all right. I know it takes time to get used to wearing it. But from now on, you must use it. We can't take chances.

BEN: Do we have to stand behind the counter even when the store's empty? Can't we sit down?
SUE: The manager says we have to stand and look ready to help anyone who comes by. He also says that there's always something to do if we just think about it.

PRACTICE USING THESE WORDS.
Find them in the conversations on page 83.
Write what they mean.   Write new sentences with them.

A.   it's all right   _____

_____

B.   to take a day off   _____

_____

C.   in that case   _____

_____

D.   to get used to   _____

_____

E.   from now on   _____

_____

F.   to take chances   _____

_____

WHAT DO YOU SAY?
Choose what you will say, line A or line B.
Only one line is the correct thing to say.

	EMPLOYEE	BOSS
1.	**A.** Excuse me, Angela. Do you have a minute? **B.** I want to talk to you, Angela.	**A.** Sure, Bob. Have a seat. What's the problem? **B.** All right, Bob. What's your problem?
2.	**A.** I'm leaving work early tomorrow. I'm picking up my mother at the airport. **B.** May I leave work early tomorrow? I have to pick up my mother at the airport.	**A.** No, you're not. You must stay. We have a report to finish by tomorrow afternoon. **B.** Of course you can leave early. But you'll have to stay late tonight. We must finish this report by tomorrow afternoon.
3.	**A.** Can't I come in early tomorrow morning? I have to go to a meeting at 6:00 tonight. **B.** I'll come in early tomorrow morning instead.	**A.** If you have to go, you can. But please be here early tomorrow. **B.** That's too bad.

Use expressions like these:

<table>
<tr><td colspan="2">ASKING ABOUT
PERMISSION/OBLIGATION</td><td>RESPONSES</td></tr>
</table>

ASKING ABOUT PERMISSION/OBLIGATION	RESPONSES
Is it all right/OK if . . . ?	Sure it is.
Do you mind if . . . ?	Certainly . . .
Are we allowed/permitted to . . . ?	Of course you can . . .
Can I . . . ? May I . . . ?	You're not allowed/permitted to . . .
Can't I . . . ?	You can't . . . You must . . .
Do I have to . . . ?	You have to . . .

A.   A new employee is talking to the boss about what is permitted on the job.

EMPLOYEE	BOSS
1. ask if you're allowed to wear jeans to work	1. not allowed
2. ask if you're permitted to take coffee breaks	2. yes; two a day
3. ask if you're allowed to leave work early if you come in early	3. no; can't leave before 5:00 without permission
4. ask if you're permitted to make personal phone calls	4. no personal calls permitted
5. ask permission to make one personal phone call a day—you have to call your children	5. agree to allow phone call to children

B.   Two busboys are talking about what they have to do on the job.

NEW EMPLOYEE	COWORKER
1. ask if you have to give menus to customers	1. no—that's the host's job
2. ask if you have to bring water to the table	2. no—that's the waiter's job
3. ask if you have to bring bread and butter to the table	3. yes; you also have to serve coffee
4. say you think that's the waiter's job	4. you can be excused from serving if you're too busy

C.   A baker asks for permission to take home two loaves of bread.

D.   An assistant asks if he/she must use a typewriter to fill out forms.

E.   A gas station attendant asks for permission to work with the mechanic. The attendant also asks if he/she must always work on weekends.

CLOSE-UP ON LANGUAGE

THE PAST TENSE OF IRREGULAR VERBS

The past tense of regular verbs is formed by adding -ed to the verb:

I work uptown now.   Last year, I worked downtown.

You don't add -ed to form the past tense of irregular verbs:

She buys all her clothes at this store.   She bought this coat a month ago.

FILL IN THE MISSING WORDS
Use the past tense. (All of these verbs are irregular.)
Use a dictionary to make a list of the irregular verbs you didn't know.

A. This letter _____ came _____ in the mail today.   (to come)

B. We _____ our telephone bill.   (to pay)

C. They _____ out the fire.   (to put)

D. The telephone _____ three times.   (to ring)

E. I _____ my umbrella at the restaurant.   (to leave)

F. I _____ her take off early.   (to let)

G. Sara _____ this sweater for me.   (to make)

H. Tony _____ that you were away.   (to know)

I. Anna _____ me a necklace from Greece.   (to bring)

J. We _____ each other at Jan's party.   (to meet)

K. I'm sorry, but I _____ your name.   (to forget)

L. He _____ a beard this summer.   (to grow)

M. The boss _____ us to take Friday off.   (to tell)

N. He _____ my coat by mistake.   (to take)

O. My mother _____ a letter to the manager.   (to write)

P. I _____ around the block.   (to run)

Q. We _____ you weren't coming.   (to think)

R. Carla _____ until noon today.   (to sleep)

S. They _____ on the corner for an hour.   (to stand)

T. No one ever _____ me how to drive a car.   (to teach)

U. You _____ you wanted to go out tonight.   (to say)

V. This shirt _____ a lot of money.   (to cost)

IRREGULAR VERBS WITH NEGATIVES

The past tense form of the main verb isn't used in negative sentences:

He <u>gave</u> Carla a present.   He didn't <u>give</u> Carla a present.

WRITE NEGATIVE SENTENCES.
Use the past tense. (All of these verbs are irregular.)
Use a dictionary to make a list of the irregular verbs you didn't know.

A.   Yoko went to the movies.

Yoko didn't go to the movies.
_____

B.   She ate dinner with us last night.

_____

C.   They got a new car.

_____

D.   We sat on the porch last night.

_____

E.   He spent thirty dollars at the store.

_____

F.   I read the paper yesterday.

_____

G.   Yoko felt sick at work.

_____

H.   They kept dinner warm for me.

_____

I.   We bought books for class.

_____

J.   He lost one of his shoes.

_____

K.   The boss gave him some advice.

_____

L.   They drove across the United States.

_____

M.   He rode to New York on a train.

_____

THE PAST PARTICIPLE OF IRREGULAR VERBS

The past participle is used:

with <u>have</u> or <u>has</u> in the present perfect tense:

I <u>have heard</u> this song on the radio.   She <u>has spoken</u> to me before.

with <u>had</u> in the past perfect tense:

He <u>had begun</u> the class when I arrived.

with <u>be</u> in the passive voice:

The house <u>was bought</u> by a young couple.

as an adjective:

The cup is <u>broken</u>.

FILL IN THE MISSING WORDS.
Use the past participle. (All of these verbs have irregular past participles.)
Make a list of the irregular verbs you didn't know. Study them on your own.

A. I was _____ hit _____ on the arm by a baseball. (to hit)

B. Her leg was _____ in an accident. (to break)

C. They had _____ the story before. (to hear)

D. Rita has _____ herself. (to cut)

E. This house was _____ in 1957. (to build)

F. She has _____ an officer at the bank. (to become)

G. The song was _____ by the band. (to sing)

H. He has _____ the package. (to send)

I. I have _____ to you about this before. (to speak)

J. He had _____ every race but the last. (to win)

K. Sharks are _____ in the ocean. (to find)

L. I have _____ the bus to work. (to ride)

M. She has _____ to learn English. (to begin)

N. That car was _____ . (to sell)

O. I had _____ worried about you. (to be)

P. I have _____ this dress many times. (to wear)

Q. Their car was _____ last week. (to steal)

R. The leaves have _____ from the trees. (to fall)

S. The money was always _____ in the safe. (to keep)

PRONOUNS

Review the forms and uses of subject, object, and possessive pronouns.

Subject Pronouns

I am buying a new car.   We live nearby.
She (He) works at Carson's.   You should call the doctor.
It was a nice day.   They are hungry.

Object Pronouns

Carla talked to me.   Kim asked us a question.
I looked for him (her).   Rita told you a story.
Tom gave it to Carl.   I saw them yesterday.

Possessive Pronouns

That's my car.   That car is mine.
Is this your coat?   Is this coat yours?
Which is her (his) house?   Which house is hers (his)?
Those are our seats.   Those seats are ours.
That's their house.   That house is theirs.
The cat likes its new toy.

FILL IN THE MISSING WORDS.
Choose the correct pronouns.

A. Did you call _____me_____ last night?   (I, me)

B. _____ told the boy to sit down.   (He, Him)

C. _____ bought some chicken for dinner.   (I, Me)

D. Sara talked to _____ yesterday.   (he, him)

E. Could you take a picture of _____ ?   (we, us)

F. _____ would like to have dinner with you.   (We, Us)

G. Shouldn't we tell _____ ?   (she, her)

H. We saw _____ at the park.   (they, them)

I. _____ is working in the store.   (She, Her)

J. Did _____ come home yet?   (they, them)

K. You and _____ should have a long talk.   (I, me)

L. This watch belongs to _____ .   (I, me)

M. Bill and _____ met at work.   (she, her)

N. Bill met _____ at work.   (she, her)

O. He made _____ a cake.   (them, they)

P. He went to the beach with _____ .   (we, us)

Q. She sent _____ a postcard.   (he, him)

R. _____ saw you on the bus.   (I, me)

REWRITE THESE SENTENCES.
Use pronouns to replace the underlined words.

A. Kwang bought a motorcycle instead of a car.

He bought a motorcycle instead of a car.

B. Jill and I have been neighbors for five years.

_____

C. Can I go with you and Lin?

_____

D. The letter was lost in the mail.

_____

E. I put the sweater in the drawer.

_____

F. Please give Carla and me your new address.

_____

G. This coat belongs to Sara.

_____

H. Alfredo and I are coworkers.

_____

I. Angela has gone to the park.

_____

J. The boss wants to talk to the employees.

_____

K. Mr. Acevedo and Ms. Chu are out of the office.

_____

L. I'm writing a letter to my brother.

_____

M. Peter told me all about you.

_____

N. Tran taught my wife and me how to drive.

_____

O. The TV has been broken since Friday.

_____

90

P. Where did you put <u>the letter</u>?

_____

Q. Say hello to <u>Bob</u> for us.

_____

R. <u>Tom</u> is working at the bank.

_____

S. <u>Robert and Carmen</u> are looking for an apartment.

_____

FILL IN THE MISSING WORDS.
Choose the correct possessive pronoun.

A. Is ___her___ leg broken?   (her, hers)

B. _____ umbrella is green, isn't it?   (Your, Yours)

C. The car behind the red one is _____ .   (my, mine)

D. You can use our telephone until you get _____ .   (your, yours)

E. Their house is next door to _____ .   (our, ours)

F. Those are _____ keys.   (my, mine)

G. Those children aren't _____ .   (her, hers)

H. Would you please take _____ picture?   (our, ours)

REWRITE THESE SENTENCES.
Use possessive pronouns.

A. Is that your book?

_____ Is that book yours? _____

B. I think that's his address.

_____

C. Her car is next to a fire hydrant.

_____

D. That's not my package.

_____

E. Which is our room?

_____

INDEFINITE PRONOUNS

Indefinite pronouns are: <u>anybody</u>, <u>anyone</u>, <u>everybody</u>, <u>everyone</u>, <u>nobody</u>, <u>no one</u>, <u>somebody</u>, and <u>someone</u>.

Did you see <u>anybody</u> (<u>anyone</u>)?   Is <u>everyone</u> (<u>everybody</u>) here?
<u>Nobody</u> (<u>no one</u>) knows what to do.   I'd like to talk to <u>someone</u> (<u>somebody</u>).

FILL IN THE MISSING WORDS.
Use an indefinite pronoun.

A. ____Everyone____ must use safety equipment on this job.

B. There is _____ at the door who wants to see you.

C. I can't find _____ who can do this.

D. There is _____ here yet.

E. Didn't _____ want a piece of this cake?

F. Please tell _____ that dinner is ready.

G. I'm afraid there's _____ here who can help you right now.

H. Is _____ missing?

I. _____ is allowed in here because it's too dangerous.

J. Does _____ remember where I put the hammer?

Indefinite pronouns take the same form of the verb as <u>he</u>, <u>she</u>, or <u>it</u>.

Has <u>anyone</u> <u>seen</u> my glasses?   <u>Everyone</u> <u>likes</u> you.
<u>No one</u> <u>wants</u> to help.   <u>Someone</u> <u>is</u> here.

FILL IN THE MISSING WORDS.
Use the correct form of the verb.

A. Everyone ____knows____ what to do, I think. (to know—present tense)

B. No one _____ seen the new house yet. (to have—present perfect tense)

C. _____ anyone want something to eat? (to do—present tense)

D. Someone _____ waiting for you. (to be—present continuous tense)

E. I don't think anybody _____ as hard as you do. (to work—present tense)

F. Everybody _____ their regards. (to send—present tense)

G. Somebody _____ to talk to you. (to want—present tense)

H. There _____ nobody at home when I got there. (to be—past tense)

92

REFLEXIVE PRONOUNS

Reflexive pronouns rename the subject of the sentence.

I looked at <u>myself</u> in the mirror. We kept to <u>ourselves</u> during the trip.
You should give <u>yourself</u> a vacation. You should take care of <u>yourselves</u>.
He burned <u>himself</u>. They bought <u>themselves</u> new clothes.
She made <u>herself</u> a cup of coffee.

With commands, <u>you</u> is understood to be the subject.

(You) Watch <u>yourself</u>.   (You) Don't hurt <u>yourselves</u>.

FILL IN THE MISSING WORDS.
Use reflexive pronouns.

A. John and his wife don't take good care of ____themselves____ .

B. Let's get _____ some coffee.

C. My mother taught _____ how to ride a bike.

D. Tom bought _____ a new set of tools.

E. I don't think I could fix it by _____ .

F. Don't hurt _____ with that knife.

G. The children make dinner for _____ when I work late.

H. I won't go out by _____ at night.

FILL IN THE MISSING WORDS.
Choose the correct pronoun.

A. Anna bought ____herself____ a new coat.   (she, herself)

B. He told _____ that he would be here at 9 o'clock.   (us, ourselves)

C. Please find some seats for _____ .   (you, yourselves)

D. Ellen sent _____ this present.   (me, myself)

E. The artist painted a picture of _____ .   (he, himself)

F. Can Nancy and I go by _____ ?   (us, ourselves)

G. Have they gotten _____ an apartment yet?   (them, themselves)

H. Will you take _____ to the movies?   (me, myself)

I. I think I'll buy _____ something to eat.   (me, myself)

J. I think Rita and Betty really enjoyed _____ .   (them, themselves)

K. Is that _____ house?   (their, themselves)

UNIT 4

ARE YOU BUSY TONIGHT?

IN THIS UNIT, YOU WILL BE:

inviting friends to go out with you

accepting and refusing invitations

reading newspaper entertainment guides

calling places for information and
    reservations

talking about what you prefer, like, and
    dislike

ordering food in a sit-down and in a fast
    food restaurant

In the Close-Up on Language, you will
review:

adjectives, adverbs, and prepositions of
    time

LOOK AT THE PICTURE.
Find these things in the picture.

1. bar
2. bartender
3. stool
4. restrooms
5. hostess
6. menu
7. booths
8. coat rack
9. salad bar
10. busboy

TALK TOPICS

LOOK AT THE PICTURE.
Talk about what you see.

What is this place?
Why do people come here?
What kind of food do you think is served
   here?

Why is the man talking to the hostess?
Why are some people sitting at the bar?
What are the workers doing?
What are the customers doing?

Do you go out to eat? How often?
Are there any restaurants in your
   neighborhood? What kinds?
What is your favorite restaurant? Where
   is it?
What kind of food do you like to order
   when you go out?
Would you rather eat at home or in a
   restaurant? Why?

What are restaurants like in your native
   country? How are they different from
   restaurants in the United States?

Pretend to be one of the people in the
   picture. What were you doing in the
   picture on page 95? What are you
   doing now? If you are talking, what
   are you saying?

ASK QUESTIONS ABOUT THE PICTURE.
Write down the new words and expressions you want to remember.

11. _____   16. _____
12. _____   17. _____
13. _____   18. _____
14. _____   19. _____
15. _____   20. _____

INVITATIONS

LISTEN TO THESE PEOPLE.
They are making plans.

ALFREDO: What are you doing tomorrow night?

RITA: I don't have any plans. Why do you ask?

ALFREDO: I thought you might like to go out to dinner with me.

RITA: I'd love to.

ALFREDO: Great. Do you like Italian food?

RITA: Yes, I do.

ALFREDO: Would 7:30 be all right?

RITA: Perfect. Where should we meet?

ALFREDO: Why don't you come over to my house? We can walk to the restaurant from here.

RITA: That's fine with me. Seven-thirty at your house—see you then.

CARMEN: Are you busy tonight?

KIM: No. I was only planning to watch TV.

CARMEN: How about going to the movies?

KIM: Sure. That would be nice. What's playing?

CARMEN: Well, there's a comedy playing at the Town Cinema, and there's a mystery at the Mall Theater. I heard that the mystery is pretty good.

KIM: Oh, I love mysteries. Let's go to that one. When does it start?

CARMEN: I don't know. I haven't called about it yet.

KIM: Would you like me to find out?

CARMEN: OK. Call me later and let me know. Then we can set a time to meet.

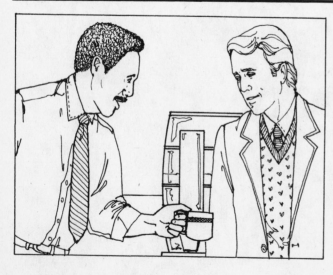

TOM: Oh, Don. We're having a party on Saturday night. Can you come?

DON: I'd like to come, but I don't think I can. I have to work on Saturday.

TOM: That's too bad. Maybe you could come after work.

DON: I'll probably be working late. I don't think I can make it.

TOM: OK. But I'll give you my address and phone number just in case. You don't have to tell me ahead of time. Just come if you can.

DON: Thanks for asking me, Tom. I can't make any promises, but I'll try to stop by.

PRACTICE USING THESE WORDS.
Find them in the conversations on page 98.
Write what they mean. Write new sentences with them.

A. see you then _____

_____

B. to find out _____

_____

C. to set a time _____

_____

D. to have a party _____

_____

E. to be able to make it _____

_____

F. just in case _____

_____

G. ahead of time _____

_____

H. to stop by _____

_____

TALK TOPICS

A. Notice how Alfredo invited Rita to go out. Notice how Carmen invited Kim to go out. Compare their invitations to Tom's invitation.
Who was direct? Who was indirect?

B. Do you think that Don answered Tom's invitation politely? Why?

C. Have you invited anyone to go out with you recently? What were you planning to do? What did you say?

D. When someone invites you out, do you think that they should pay for your entertainment?

E. What are some more formal ways of inviting someone? Have you ever received a written invitation? What did it say?

F. What is dating like in your native country? How is it different from dating in the United States?

G. Have you ever been to a party in the United States? What was it like?

LOOK AT THIS ENTERTAINMENT GUIDE.
Answer the questions.

SATURDAY AROUND THE TOWN

Community Board

FAMILY FUN DAY, clowns, pony rides, balloons, races, games for all ages, Great Park, 1.

BAZAAR, sponsored by the Women's Auxiliary of the Fire Dept., Fire Station, 10–5.

3rd ANNUAL FIREFIGHTERS' SPAGHETTI DINNER, all you can eat, Fire Station, 5–9.

Y DANCE, sponsored by the Youth Council, with a deejay from WJMR, Tate High School, 75 Tate Rd., 8.

THE GOOD LIFE, a play, Community Playhouse, 17 River Dr., 8.

FLEA MARKET, outside Town Hall, 12.

Music

KIRBY JOLLY'S LITTLE BRASS BAND, free concert, The Meadow, 8.

STANLEY DAVIS, jazz, The Green Parrot, 17 Rice St., 9, 12.

THE BANDITS, country/rock, Grass Roots, 567 Central Ave., 8:30, 11.

Arts

CRAFTS SHOW, pottery, rugs, needlework, jewelry, Tate High School, 10–4.

REGIONAL ARTISTS, painters and sculptors from the area, R. J. Stevens Gallery, 542 Central Ave., 11.

Movies

MALL THEATER—"The Golden Clue," PG, 1:25, 3:35, 5:40, 8, 10:10.

PLAZA TWIN—
I—"Fun Times in Flatbush," G, 1, 3:20, 5:35, 7:45.
II—"It Happened to Me," PG, 1, 3:10, 5:15, 7:20, 9:40

TOWN CINEMA—"Those Crazy Kids," PG, 2, 3:55, 5:50, 7:40, 9:45

TRIANGLE THEATER—
I—"Those Crazy Kids," PG, 1:40, 3:45, 5:50, 7:55
II—"Starship II," G, 2, 4, 6, 8, 10.
III—"The Bride Wore Blood," R, 1, 3, 5, 7, 9.

A. Where is "Family Fun Day" being held? When does it begin?
B. What time does the bazaar at the fire station begin?
C. How long will the spaghetti dinner last? What does "all you can eat" mean?
D. Where is the Y dance? What is a "deejay"?
E. What is "The Good Life"? Where can you see it?
F. What is a "flea market"? Where can you find one?
G. Do you have to pay to hear Kirby Jolly's Little Brass Band? When will the music begin?
H. What kind of music does Stanley Davis play? Where is he playing?
I. What kind of music do The Bandits play? When are they playing?
J. What kinds of art exhibits are listed?
K. Look at the movie listing. What do the letters "G," "PG," and "R," mean? Do these ratings help you choose a movie?
L. What is the rating of "Those Crazy Kids"? It is showing at the Town Cinema and the Triangle Theater.
M. What movies can you see at the Triangle Theater?
N. You missed the 3:10 show of "It Happened to Me" at Plaza Twin II. What time is the next show? What time will that show end?

TRY IT IN CLASS.
Practice with another student.
Two friends are making plans to go out together.
Use the entertainment guide on page 100 in dialogues A, C, and D.

Use expressions like these:

INVITING SOMEONE

Would you like to . . . ?
How about . . . ?
Why don't we . . . ?
I thought you might . . .
Want to . . . ?
Can you . . . ?
Are you busy . . . ?
Do you have any plans . . . ?

RESPONDING TO AN INVITATION

I'd love/like to . . .
That would be nice . . .
Sounds great/good.

Sorry, I can't make it.
I'd like to, but . . .
Maybe some other time.
Could we make it another time?
I can't make it on _____ , but how about _____ ?

A. Two friends are making plans to go dancing.

FRIEND A

1. ask friend to go to the Y dance

2. give the time; ask where to meet
3. agree; give your address

FRIEND B

1. accept—you like to dance; ask when dance starts
2. meet at friend's house
3. thank friend for asking you to dance

B. A person is inviting a friend to dinner.

FRIEND A

1. ask friend to your house for dinner tonight
2. ask if friend would prefer to eat steak or chicken for dinner
3. give a time

FRIEND B

1. you'd like to go

2. tell which you prefer; ask what time to come over
3. thank friend

C. A person is inviting a friend to go to the Crafts Show.

FRIEND A

1. ask friend to go to show
2. give time

FRIEND B

1. accept; ask when
2. you can't go then—you're busy; you want to go another day

D. Choose an activity from the Entertainment Guide. Invite another student to go with you.

LISTEN TO THESE PEOPLE.
They are calling for information about a show.

OPERATOR: Community Playhouse. Good afternoon.

LEE: Good afternoon. I'd like some information about <u>The Good Life</u>.

OPERATOR: There's a show at 8:00 tonight and a matinee tomorrow at 1:00.

LEE: How much are the tickets?

OPERATOR: Tickets are $5.00 apiece.

LEE: Do you have reserved seating?

OPERATOR: Yes, we do. Where would you like to sit?

LEE: Do you have any seats left in the balcony? I need three.

OPERATOR: Yes. Your name, please?

LEE: It's Wong. W-O-N-G.

OPERATOR: OK, Mr. Wong. I'll put aside three tickets for you.

OPERATOR: The Green Parrot.

ANNA: Can you give me some information about the music tonight?

OPERATOR: Certainly. What would you like to know?

ANNA: Who's playing and what time are the performances?

OPERATOR: We've got Stanley Davis tonight. He's playing from 9 until 11 and from 12 until 2.

ANNA: Is there a cover charge?

OPERATOR: Yes. The cover charge is $4.00.

ANNA: Can I reserve a table?

OPERATOR: No, we don't take reservations. It's best to get here early.

ANNA: Thanks.

TALK TOPICS

A. What is a "matinee"? What is "reserved seating"?

B. What does it mean to "have seats left in the balcony"?
What does it mean to "put aside three tickets"?

C. Have you ever seen a play in the United States? What was it like?
How was it different from a play performed in your native country?

D. What is a "cover charge"?

E. Are there places to hear "live" music in your community?
What kind of music do you like?

TRY IT IN CLASS.
Practice with another student.
One person is working at the Triangle Theater.
The other person is calling the theater for information.

The theater employee should use this information:

Theater I—Those Crazy Kids, rated PG (parental guidance advised)
1:40, 3:45, 5:50, 7:55
Theater II—Starship II, rated G (general audiences)
2:00, 4:00, 6:00, 8:00, 10:00
Theater III—The Bride Wore Blood, rated R (no one under 17 admitted without adult)
1:00, 3:00, 5:00, 7:00, 9:00

Ticket prices are $4.50 for adults and $3.00 for children under 12.

A. A person is calling for information about Those Crazy Kids.

OPERATOR	CALLER
1. answer phone	1. ask for movie times after 6:00
2. give times	2. ask if movie is OK for children to see
3. tell about rating	3. ask how much adult's ticket costs
4. give price	4. thank operator

B. A person is calling for information about Starship II.

OPERATOR	CALLER
1. answer phone	1. ask for movie times before 5:00
2. give times	2. ask if movie is OK for children to see
3. tell about rating	3. ask how much adult's ticket and child's ticket cost
4. give prices	4. thank operator

C. A person is calling for information about The Bride Wore Blood.

OPERATOR	CALLER
1. answer phone	1. ask for movie times—day and night
2. give times	2. ask if child can see movie
3. tell about rating	3. ask how much adult's ticket costs
4. give price	4. thank operator

D. Bring in a movie listing from your newspaper. One student should be the operator at a local theater. The other student should call the operator for information.

TALKING ABOUT PREFERENCES

LISTEN TO THESE PEOPLE.
They are talking about what they would prefer to do.

CARMEN: Do you feel like going for a bite to eat?

KIM: OK. Let's go to Mario's. I like their lasagna.

CARMEN: Yes, I like it too. But I'd rather not eat pasta. I had it for lunch today.

KIM: You could get chicken or a salad there. Or we could go to another restaurant instead.

CARMEN: I'd prefer to go to another place. Mario's is too far away. Have you ever been to the Odyssey? Their specialty is shish kebab.

KIM: I don't care for shish kebab. Why don't we go to the Royal Diner? They serve both lasagna and shish kebab. It's only a block away.

CARMEN: That's fine with me.

TOM: Want to get something to eat?

NANCY: Sure. What do you have in mind?

TOM: Let's see. I'd like a steak and some salad. Do you want to go to Beefy's?

NANCY: I don't really like Beefy's very much. It's always so noisy and crowded. How about the Leatherman Inn instead?

TOM: It's too fancy for me. I'd rather go someplace more casual and less expensive.

NANCY: OK. Do you like Fern's Place?

TOM: I've never been there before. What's it like?

NANCY: It's kind of casual. You can get sandwiches or entrees. And their prices are reasonable.

TOM: All right. I'll give it a try.

PRACTICE USING THESE WORDS.
Find them in the conversations.
Write what they mean. Write new sentences with them.

A. a bite to eat _____

_____

B. to care for (something) _____

_____

C. that's fine with me _____

_____

D. to give (something/someplace) a try _____

_____

104

READING RESTAURANT ADS

Look at these ads. Then answer the questions.

Mario's Restaurant

FEATURING...
our world-famous lasagna
823-6778

Open 7 days a week from noon 'til 2 A.M.
300 Park St.

"when you'd rather have the best"

Royal Diner

★ Italian
★ Greek
★ American

We're always open & we deliver

4 Main St.   825-9878

The Leatherman Inn
Fine Dining Since 1870

Lunch
Cocktails
Dinner

71 Old Country Road
Reservations 823-7562
All Major Credit Cards Accepted

The Odyssey

Great Greek Food at a Reasonable Price

SHISH KEBAB OUR SPECIALTY

15 Main St. (Located in the heart of town)
825-0172

steak lovers prefer...
BEEFY'S
FAMILY RESTAURANT

free salad bar with dinner
85 York Ave.   823-1763

Fern's Place

at the corner of York and Main

825-5647

Open Daily—11 a.m.–2 a.m.

Join us for Sunday Brunch

CHINA SEA
AUTHENTIC CHINESE CUISINE

2 dining rooms • take-out • free delivery
250 Park St.

823-4257

A. Sometimes ads give us a clue to price. Can you guess how expensive these restaurants are?

B. What is "cuisine"? What is a "specialty"? Talk about the kinds of food served at these restaurants.

C. It's 11 o'clock on Sunday morning. Can you eat at Mario's? Can you eat at Fern's Place? Can you eat at the Royal Diner?

D. If you go to Beefy's and only order a salad, will your meal be free?

E. Look at the ad for "Fern's Place." What is "brunch"? What foods are usually served at brunch?

F. Look at the ad for China Sea. What is "take-out"? What is "free delivery"?

G. Look at the ad for The Leatherman Inn. What does "all major credit cards accepted" mean?

Practice with another student.

Use expressions like these:

ASKING FOR PREFERENCES	**STATING PREFERENCES**
Do you feel like . . . ?	I'd rather . . .
Do you want to . . . ?	I'd rather not . . .
Want to . . . ?	I'd prefer . . .
Do you like . . . ?	I don't care for . . .
Why don't we . . . ?	We could . . . instead
How about . . . ?	Let's go . . . instead
What do you have in mind?	

A. A person (Friend B) is watching TV at a friend's house. They are trying to decide what to eat.

FRIEND A	**FRIEND B**
1. ask if friend wants to eat	1. yes, you do
2. suggest that you order a pizza from the Royal Diner	2. you don't like pizza—you want Chinese food; suggest calling the Hunan House
3. that restaurant doesn't deliver; ask if friend likes the China Sea	3. you like the China Sea; agree to order from there

B. Two friends are trying to decide where to eat dinner.

FRIEND A	**FRIEND B**
1. ask if friend likes Greek food	1. you like Greek food; ask friend to suggest a Greek restaurant
2. you like The Odyssey	2. you think that The Odyssey is too expensive; you want to go to a diner
3. suggest the Royal Diner	3. agree to go to the Royal Diner

C. Two friends are trying to decide where to eat lunch.

FRIEND A	**FRIEND B**
1. ask if friend wants to go out to lunch	1. you'd like to; ask where
2. you like Fern's Place	2. you don't like Fern's Place—it's too crowded; suggest Mario's
3. you don't want Italian food— suggest The Leatherman Inn	3. you'll try to make a reservation

D. Decide with another student where to go for dinner. Choose from the restaurants given on page 105.

ORDERING FOOD AT A RESTAURANT

LISTEN TO THESE PEOPLE.
They are ordering at a restaurant.

MARY: What are you having, Peter?
PETER: Oh, I can't decide. What are you having?
MARY: I think I'll get the shrimp. And maybe some soup to start.
PETER: Shrimp sounds delicious. But I'm in the mood for a thick juicy steak.
MARY: Why don't you have the Surf 'n Turf? Then you can have both steak and shrimp.
PETER: That's an excellent suggestion. I'll have that.
MARY: Excuse me, waiter!
WAITER: Yes?
MARY: We're ready to order now.
WAITER: I'll be right with you, ma'am.

WAITER: Are you ready to order now?
OSCAR: I think so. Have you decided, Ann?
ANN: Yes. I'll have the sirloin steak.
WAITER: How would you like that?
ANN: Medium, please.
WAITER: Would you like a baked potato or french fries with that?
ANN: Baked, with some sour cream on the side.
WAITER: What would you like to drink?
ANN: Ginger ale.
WAITER: OK. Thank you. Please help yourself to the salad bar. And what are you having, sir?
OSCAR: What's the soup of the day?
WAITER: It's pea soup.
OSCAR: I'll have a cup of that. I'd also like a chef's salad.
WAITER: Anything to drink?
OSCAR: Just water, please.
WAITER: Thank you.

TALK TOPICS

A. Look at what the waiter said to Mary. What does "I'll be right with you" mean?
B. What does "soup to start" mean?
C. What does it mean to say that shrimp "sounds delicious"?
D. What does it mean to "be in the mood" for something?
E. What does it mean to "help yourself" to something?

THE GOLDEN EAGLE RESTAURANT

1756 Mountain Avenue
246-0800

Appetizers

melon (in season)............	$1.50
grapefruit half..............	.75
tomato juice	.75
shrimp cocktail	2.50
baked clams	2.50

Soups

onion soup au gratin.........................	$2.00
cream of mushroom...........................	1.25
seafood chowder	2.50
soup of the day cup	.85
bowl	1.50

Sandwiches

hamburger	$2.75
cheeseburger	3.00
club (ham, turkey, cheese)	3.50
roast beef	3.25
fried filet of fish	2.50
grilled cheese................	2.00
tuna fish	2.15
shrimp salad.................	2.75
chicken salad................	2.50

Entrees

	a la carte	dinner
roast chicken	$ 4.25	$ 6.25
broiled flounder	5.95	7.95
broiled shrimp	8.95	10.95
roast prime rib	9.95	11.95
london broil	6.50	8.50
sirloin steak	9.50	11.50
lamb roast.......................	9.95	11.50
surf 'n turf (sirloin and shrimp)	11.50	13.50

All dinner entrees are served with a baked potato or french fries, bread and butter, and include unlimited salad from our Super Salad Bar.

LOOK AT THE MENU.
Answer the questions.

A. Do you know what all these foods are? Talk about the ones you're unsure of.
B. What is an "appetizer"? What is a "side order"? What is an "entree"?
C. Look at the soup list. Which is larger, a cup of soup or a bowl of soup? When you order onion soup, cream of mushroom soup, or seafood chowder, can you choose between a cup and a bowl?
D. Look at the salad list. How much does salad (salad bar) cost if you don't order a sandwich or an entree? How much does salad (salad bar) cost if you order a sandwich?
Do you usually like to have a salad with a meal?
E. Look at the entree list. What is the difference between a "dinner" and "a la carte"? What do you get when you order a dinner? What do you get when you order a la carte?
If you wanted only flounder and french fries, is it cheaper to order a dinner or a la carte?
If you wanted flounder, french fries, and salad (salad bar), is it cheaper to order a dinner or a la carte?
F. Look at the dessert list. What kinds of pie can you get? What kinds of cake can you get?

Beverages

coffee	$.50
tea	.50
hot chocolate	.75
milk	.60
sodas	.70

Salads

spinach	$2.50
chef's	3.00
salad bar as a meal	3.95
salad bar (w/sandwich or entree)	1.50

Side Orders

french fries	$.75
onion rings	.75

Carry Out All the menu items can be packaged "to go." Stop by our carry-out counter or call in your order.

Desserts

pie (apple, cherry, peach)	$1.25
cheese cake	1.50
chocolate layer cake	1.50
carrot cake	1.25
strawberry shortcake	1.50
ice cream	.75

G. Are there any foods on this menu that you can't eat? What, if anything, would you order if you went to this restaurant?

H. What is "carry-out"? Does The Golden Eagle have carry-out? Can you place an order by phone?

TRY IT IN CLASS.
Practice with another student.

A. Two friends are dining together at the Golden Eagle. Talk about what you're going to order. Choose an appetizer, a dinner entree, a dessert, and a beverage.

B. A customer at the Golden Eagle is ordering his/her food. The customer should choose soup of the day, a dinner entree, and a beverage. The waitress/waiter should ask the customer questions (such as "Would you like a cup or a bowl of soup?").

C. A customer is calling in an order at the Golden Eagle. The customer orders a hamburger, a cheeseburger, and two side orders of french fries. The waiter/waitress tells the customer how much the food will cost (free delivery–no tax).

COMPLAINING AT A RESTAURANT

LISTEN TO THESE PEOPLE.
They are talking about problems with the food and service in a restaurant.

KIM: Where's our food? The service in this place is really slow.

DAN: They seem to be very busy today. I'm sure the waitress didn't forget our order.

KIM: I'm going to ask our waitress to hurry things up. I'm never coming to this restaurant again.

DAN: Relax, Kim. We're not in a hurry. Our food will be here soon.

LEE: Pardon me, waitress. What happened to my order?

WAITRESS: It should be ready any minute, sir.

LEE: What's holding it up? I gave you my order over twenty minutes ago.

WAITRESS: I'm sorry. We're very busy.

LEE: I hate to complain, but I'm on my lunch hour. Do you think you could speed things up?

WAITRESS: I'll do my best, sir.

FRED: Oh, this steak is well-done. Didn't I order it rare?

ANN: I think so, Fred. Send it back.

FRED: No, I'll eat it anyway. It just won't taste as good.

ANN: Let's get the waiter. I'm sure he'd be happy to bring you another steak.

FRED: OK. But don't let your meal get cold.

MARTA: Oh, waiter? This soup is cold. Could you have it warmed up?

WAITER: Certainly. I'm terribly sorry. This doesn't happen very often.

MARTA: Don't worry about it. There's no rush. Take your time.

WAITER: Can I bring some more bread and butter while you're waiting?

MARTA: That would be nice. Thank you.

PRACTICE USING THESE WORDS.
Find them in the conversations on page 110.
Write what they mean. Write new sentences with them.

A. to hurry (something) up _____

_____

B. to be in a hurry _____

_____

C. to send (something) back _____

_____

D. to speed things up _____

_____

E. to warm (something) up _____

_____

TRY IT IN CLASS.
Practice with another student.

A. Two friends are having lunch together. One of them (Friend A) is complaining because the restaurant is too cold.

FRIEND A	**FRIEND B**
1. complain to friend that you're cold	**1.** offer to give friend your sweater
2. suggest that you move to another table—away from air conditioner	**2.** agree to move; call waitress

B. A customer is complaining to the waiter. The customer doesn't like his/her food.

CUSTOMER	**WAITER**
1. call waiter	**1.** ask to help customer
2. your fish tastes bad; you don't like it	**2.** apologize about fish; offer to bring customer something else
3. agree; ask to see menu again	**3.** tell customer that you'll get menu

C. A customer is complaining to the waiter. The customer says that he/she ordered fried chicken. The waiter served the customer broiled chicken. The customer is in a hurry. The waiter tries to fix the mistake.

POINTING OUT MISTAKES

LISTEN TO THESE PEOPLE.
They are pointing out mistakes on their bills.

ALFREDO: I think you've made a mistake on my bill.
WAITER: Really? What's wrong with it?
ALFREDO: You overcharged me. The broiled shrimp is $10.95, and you wrote $11.95 on the bill.
WAITER: Did I? I'm terribly sorry. Let me correct it for you.

ANITA: May I have another look at the menu?
WAITER: Certainly. Is something wrong?
ANITA: I'm not sure. You charged me extra for the french fries, and I thought they came with the club sandwich.
WAITER: No, madam. There's an extra charge for french fries with a sandwich. They're only free with an entree.
ANITA: Oh, I see. I didn't realize that before.

YUKI: Excuse me, waitress. There's an error on my bill.
WAITRESS: There is?
YUKI: Yes. You added it up wrong. It should come to $12.25, but the total here is $13.25.
WAITRESS: Oh, I'm sorry. I'll fix it right now.
YUKI: That's all right.

CHECKING A BILL

Look at this bill from the Golden Eagle Restaurant. Answer the questions.
(Use the menu on pages 108–109 to check the prices.)

GUEST CHECK	
1 tomato juice	.75
2 cream of mushroom soups	4.00
1 sirloin steak dinner	11.50
1 surf 'n turf dinner	13.00
2 coffees	1.00
TOTAL	$30.25

A. What are the mistakes on this bill?
B. What will the diner say to the waiter or waitress?
C. What will the waiter or waitress say?
D. What will the waiter or waitress do to correct the bill?
E. What will the correct total be?

TIPPING

LISTEN TO THESE PEOPLE.
They are talking about leaving a tip.

CARMEN: How much should we leave for the tip?
KIM: I think you're supposed to leave about fifteen percent of the total.
CARMEN: The bill comes to $8.00. What's fifteen percent of that?
KIM: Let me see. It's a dollar twenty.
CARMEN: I've got a dollar bill. Do you have any change?
KIM: Here's a quarter.
CARMEN: That's good. Let's go.

TALK TOPICS

Answer these questions in class.

A. What is a "tip"?
B. Name some other people (such as taxi drivers) who receive tips in the U.S.
C. How much tip (what percent) do you usually leave?
D. Do people tip in your native country? Who do they tip? How much money do they tip?

TIPS ON TIPPING

Fifteen percent (15%) of the total is the average tip in most places.
Here is an easy way to figure out the tip:

A. Take ten percent of the total: 10% of $8.00 = $.80
B. Take five percent of the total:
   (half of ten percent):   5% of $8.00 (½ of $.80) = $.40
C. Add the ten percent and the five percent: 10% ($.80) + 5% ($.40) = $1.20

TRY IT IN CLASS.
Practice with another student. One student figures out the tip.
The other student tells which bills and change they could use for the tip.

A. The total bill is $10.00.
B. The total bill is $6.00.
C. The total bill is $36.40.
D. The total bill is $20.80.
E. The total bill is $2.40.

FAST FOOD RESTAURANTS

TALK TOPICS.
Answer these questions in class.

A. Look at the picture. Where do you order your food? Where can you eat your food?

B. How is this restaurant different from the restaurant pictured on pages 94–97?

C. Look at the menu. What do you think a "Cheese Magic" is? What is a "Double Cheese Magic"? a "Fish Magic"? a "Chicken Magic"?

D. Do you think that fast food is good for you? Why?

E. Are there any foods on the "Magic Burger" menu that you can't eat?

F. Are there any fast food restaurants in your native country? If so, do many people go to them?

LISTEN TO THESE PEOPLE.
They are ordering at a fast food restaurant.

COUNTERPERSON: Can I help you?
MIKE: I'll take a Cheese Magic with lettuce and tomato.
COUNTERPERSON: Anything to drink?
MIKE: Coffee, please. Black.
COUNTERPERSON: For here or to go?
MIKE: To go, please.
COUNTERPERSON: Cheese Magic, tomato and lettuce, and coffee. That comes to $2.25.
MIKE: Here's three dollars.
COUNTERPERSON: Do you have a quarter? We're pretty low on change.
MIKE: Let's see. Yes, I do. Here you are.
COUNTERPERSON: And here's a dollar.

COUNTERPERSON: Next?
TERESA: Two magic burgers; two small orders of fries.
COUNTERPERSON: What to drink?
TERESA: A large cola and a small vanilla shake, please.
COUNTERPERSON: To eat here or to take out?
TERESA: We'll eat here.
COUNTERPERSON: That'll be $5.50.
TERESA: Here you go.
COUNTERPERSON: Five thirty out of six. Here's your change. Who's next?

TRY IT IN CLASS.
Practice with another student.

A. A customer is ordering food at Magic Burger.

COUNTERPERSON	**CUSTOMER**
1. ask to help customer	1. order a Fish Magic
2. ask what customer wants to drink	2. order a cola
3. ask if customer wants a large or small cola	3. you want a large cola
4. ask where customer is eating food	4. you want to eat in restaurant
5. tell customer total price	5. give counterperson $3.00
6. count out change; thank customer	6. thank counterperson

B. A customer is ordering at Chicken Magic. The counterperson takes the customer's order and gives the customer change.

C. A customer is ordering food at Magic Burger (choose anything on the menu). The counterperson takes the customer's order.

THANKS FOR ASKING ME

LISTEN TO THESE PEOPLE.
They are saying goodbye to each other.

FRED: It was a great party, Ann. Thanks for inviting me.
ANN: You're very welcome, Fred. I enjoyed having you. I hope you'll come again.
FRED: I'd love to. Oh, Ann, I'm thinking about having some people over to my house for dinner next week. Do you think you can come?
ANN: Sure. Give me a call when you've set the date.
FRED: Good. Thanks again.

RITA: This was a fun evening, Yung. I'm glad you asked me to come.
YUNG: I enjoyed it, too. We'll have to get together again sometime.
RITA: I'd like that. Good night.

TALK TOPICS

A. How do people in your native country thank each other for an invitation? Do they send a gift or write a note?
B. What does "having people over" mean?
C. What does "set the date" mean?
D. What does "get together" mean?

CLOSE-UP ON LANGUAGE

ADJECTIVE OR ADVERB?

Adjectives describe nouns and pronouns.
They tell <u>what kind</u>, <u>how much</u>, or <u>how many</u>.
Notice that these adjectives come before the nouns they describe:

<blockquote>He is a <u>kind</u> man.   I've got <u>two new</u> scarves.</blockquote>

Adjectives do not always come before the nouns they describe.
Notice that these adjectives follow a verb:

<blockquote>That man is <u>kind</u>.   These two scarves are <u>new</u>.</blockquote>

Adverbs describe verbs. They tell <u>how</u>, <u>where</u>, or <u>when</u>.
Like adjectives, some adverbs follow a verb:

<blockquote>He walked <u>slowly</u>.   She was <u>seriously</u> hurt.</blockquote>

Many adverbs are formed by adding <u>-ly</u> to adjectives:

<blockquote>ADJECTIVE: Please be <u>careful</u>.   ADVERB: Do this <u>carefully</u>.</blockquote>

FILL IN THE MISSING WORDS.
Choose an adjective to describe a noun.
Choose an adverb to describe a verb.

A. The child has _____soft_____ skin. (soft, softly)

B. The man sang _____ to himself. (soft, softly)

C. Look _____ at this picture. (close, closely)

D. The doctor took a _____ look at my eyes. (close, closely)

E. This car is _____ . (cheap, cheaply)

F. This cake is _____ . (sweet, sweetly)

G. The doctor arrived _____ after we called. (short, shortly)

H. We had a _____ meeting today. (short, shortly)

I. Carla types _____ . (quick, quickly)

J. I took a _____ walk before dinner. (quick, quickly)

K. He cut himself _____ . (bad, badly)

L. The service in the restaurant was _____ . (bad, badly)

M. The baby was _____ all night. (quiet, quietly)

N. She was reading _____ when the phone rang. (quiet, quietly)

O. He looked _____ at his wife.   (sad, sadly)

P. She seemed _____ .   (sad, sadly)

Q. Please drive _____ .   (careful, carefully)

R. He was _____ at the waiter.   (angry, angrily)

S. He spoke _____ .   (angry, angrily)

T. They smiled _____ .   (happy, happily)

U. They seemed _____ .   (happy, happily)

V. The waitress was very _____ .   (slow, slowly)

W. He ate _____ .   (slow, slowly)

Some words act as both adjectives and adverbs.

ADJECTIVE   We watched the late show.

ADVERB   She came late to class.

REWRITE THESE SENTENCES.
Use the word on the right as an adverb.
Add -ly when necessary.

A. Yung types.   (fast)

<u>   Yung types fast.   </u>

B. Carmen types.   (quick)

_____

C. The guests arrived.   (late)

_____

D. She hurt herself.   (bad)

_____

E. We tried to win the game.   (hard)

_____

F. She was injured in the fire.   (serious)

_____

G. Everyone left the party.   (early)

_____

H. They talked to each other.   (loud)

_____

COMPARISONS

To compare two things, use the comparative forms of adjectives and adverbs:

ADJECTIVES   Alfredo is <u>taller</u> than Roberto.
                This book is <u>more interesting</u> than that one.
ADVERBS   Sara runs <u>faster</u> than Mary.
                I drive <u>more carefully</u> than you.

To compare three or more things, use the superlative forms of adjectives and adverbs:

ADJECTIVES   The Royal Diner is the <u>cheapest</u> restaurant in town.
                The Leatherman Inn is the <u>most expensive</u> restaurant in town.
ADVERBS   Angela tried the <u>hardest</u> to win.

Notice that these adjectives and adverbs have irregular comparative and superlative forms:

bad(ly)	worse	worst
good (well)	better	best

WRITE COMPARATIVE SENTENCES.
Compare the two things.

A. a sportscar that costs $5,000   a van that costs $3,500

_____The sportscar is more expensive than the van._____ (expensive)

B. Bill—25 years old   Jane—43 years old

_____ (old)

C. ice cream—150 calories   apple—50 calories

_____ (fattening)

D. Tom gets up at 6:00.   Rick gets up at 5:30.

_____ (early)

E. This line has 4 people in it.   That line has 8 people in it.

_____ (long)

F. Kim types 60 words per minute.   Oscar types 55 words per minute.

_____ (fast)

G. Tran worked 5 hours.   Kwang worked 8 hours.

_____ (long)

H. Lin—5'2"   Marta—5'6"

_____ (short)

119

FILL IN THE MISSING WORDS.

A. Yesterday was the _____ day of the year. (cold)

B. Fred is the _____ person in class. (friendly)

C. This book is the _____ book I have ever read. (good)

D. Nancy is the _____ woman in the room. (attractive)

E. This is the _____ room in the house. (large)

F. Rita is the _____ person I know. (smart)

G. This restaurant has the _____ service in town. (bad)

H. Kim is the _____ student in class. (young)

FILL IN THE MISSING WORDS.
Use the superlative or the comparative form of the adjective or adverb given.

A. That's the ___biggest___ house in the neighborhood. (big)

B. Marta sings _____ than you do. (bad)

C. That's the _____ dress in the store. (pretty)

D. This blouse is _____ than that one. (cheap)

E. Who's the _____ person in your family? (tall)

F. Is hamburger _____ than chicken? (expensive)

G. Which restaurant has _____ food, Beefy's or Arty's? (good)

H. This painting is _____ than that one. (beautiful)

I. He is the _____ typist in the office. (fast)

J. Yung is the _____ driver on the road. (careful)

K. Betty is the _____ person I know. (quiet)

L. Tom works _____ than Dan. (quick)

M. Lan is _____ than his brother. (old)

N. This room is _____ than that one. (large)

O. Ann is the _____ cashier in the supermarket. (slow)

P. Fern's Place is the _____ restaurant in town. (popular)

Q. This is the _____ test in the book. (hard)

R. This candy is _____ than that cake. (sweet)

S. The onion soup is _____ than the clam chowder. (delicious)

T. Bicycling is _____ than jogging. (fun)

Here are some other ways to compare two things:

Plain yogurt is <u>less fattening than</u> flavored yogurt.
Plain yogurt is <u>not as fattening as</u> flavored yogurt.
Plain yogurt tastes <u>as good as</u> flavored yogurt.

REWRITE THESE SENTENCES.
Use <u>less . . . than</u>, <u>not as . . . as</u>, or <u>as . . . as</u>.

A. This shelf is 5 feet high. That shelf is 6 feet high.

This shelf is not as tall as that shelf. (tall)

B. The blue shirt costs $40.00. The red shirt costs $25.00.

_____ (expensive)

C. The weather yesterday was bad. The weather today is worse.

_____ (bad)

D. I think that swimming is hard. I think that running is also hard.

_____ (hard)

E. This brand of cough syrup is powerful. That brand of cough syrup is also powerful.

_____ (powerful)

F. One cup of spinach has 45 calories. One cup of peas has 110 calories.

_____ (fattening)

G. This play is good. That play is better.

_____ (good)

H. Laura is 5 feet 8 inches tall. Dan is 5 feet 8 inches tall.

_____ (tall)

I. His mortgage payment is $300.00 a month. Her mortgage payment is $300 a month.

_____ (high)

J. Maria is strong. Kim is strong.

_____ (strong)

K. This package weighs 5 lbs. That package weighs 5 lbs.

_____ (heavy)

L. Oscar jogs once a week. Lee jogs once a week.

_____ (often)

COMPARING QUANTITIES

Use as many . . . as or as much . . . as to compare amounts.

As many . . . as is used to compare things that can be counted:

He ate as many cookies as she did.   He didn't walk as many miles as she did.

As much . . . as is used to compare things that cannot be counted:

He ate as much food as she did.   He didn't do as much exercise as she did.

COMPARE THE TWO AMOUNTS.

A.   Lin spent $25.00.   Yoko spend $38.00.

_____ Lin didn't spend as much money as Yoko. _____

B.   Playing tennis uses 7 calories a minute.   Swimming uses 7 calories a minute.

_____

C.   This recipe calls for a cup of milk.   That recipe calls for a cup of milk.

_____

D.   Rita ran 5 miles.   Yung ran 5 miles.

_____

E.   Butter—100 calories   Mayonnaise—100 calories

_____

F.   This bottle contains 40 capsules.   That bottle contains 50 capsules.

_____

G.   Our apartment has 4 rooms.   Their apartment has 5 rooms.

_____

H.   This tube contains 8 oz. of cream.   That tube contains 8 oz. of cream.

_____

I.   Carla slept 7 hours.   Roberto slept 7 hours.

_____

J.   Carmen talked to 9 people today.   George talked to 9 people today.

_____

K.   This cereal contains sugar.   That cereal contains the same amount of sugar.

_____

HOW OFTEN?

These adverbs tell how often something happens: <u>never</u>, <u>rarely</u>, <u>seldom</u>, <u>hardly ever</u>, <u>sometimes</u>, <u>often</u>, <u>usually</u>, <u>always</u>.

> I <u>never</u> drink tea.   I don't like it.
> I <u>rarely</u> eat meat.   It's not on my diet.
> I am <u>seldom</u> tired.   I <u>usually</u> get enough sleep.
> I <u>hardly ever</u> go to the movies.   There aren't many movies that I like.
> I <u>sometimes</u> have trouble sleeping.
> I am <u>often</u> late for appointments.   I <u>usually</u> keep people waiting.
> I <u>always</u> drink coffee.   I like it.

FILL IN THE MISSING WORDS.
Choose the correct adverb.

A. I'm ____often____ tired; I don't get enough sleep.   (often, seldom)

B. Carla _____ goes out, but not very often.   (rarely, sometimes)

C. Kwang _____ drinks milk because he doesn't like it.   (always, never)

D. Lee _____ watches TV because he doesn't like the shows.   (often, rarely)

E. Roberto _____ buys steak—it's too expensive.   (always, hardly ever)

F. He _____ runs every day because he likes to feel healthy.   (always, rarely)

G. We _____ have breakfast every morning.   (sometimes, usually)

H. Anna _____ uses sugar because she's on a low-sugar diet.   (rarely, usually)

I. Peter _____ walks to work because it's far away.   (seldom, usually)

J. Tran _____ goes to restaurants; she eats at home.   (always, never)

K. Marta _____ eats fish because it makes her sick.   (never, sometimes)

L. George _____ takes the train because he doesn't drive.   (often, seldom)

M. Don is _____ at home because he is always at work.   (hardly ever, often)

N. I _____ eat hamburgers because I don't like them.   (rarely, usually)

O. Tom is a good employee because he _____ misses work.   (always, never)

P. I never shop at Baker's Market; I _____ go to Shop Wise.   (always, seldom)

Q. I always used to watch TV, but now I _____ do.   (seldom, usually)

R. I _____ drive; I don't know how.   (never, usually)

S. She's _____ sick; she's very healthy.   (often, rarely)

T. They're _____ on time; they're never late.   (always, never)

U. We _____ eat at restaurants because we don't cook.   (seldom, usually)

HOW LONG?

These prepositions are used to talk about time: for, since.

Use for to talk about a length of time:

I've been sick for a few weeks.

Use since to talk about a specific point in time something started:

That restaurant has been open since Friday.

FILL IN THE MISSING WORDS.
Use for or since.

A. She's been out _____since_____ noon.

B. We have been waiting _____ an hour.

C. We have been living here _____ May.

D. He has been working here _____ three years.

E. That restaurant has been closed _____ September.

F. This TV show has been on _____ eight o'clock.

G. I've been shopping _____ two hours.

H. He's been busy _____ several days.

I. They've been away _____ six months.

J. I've had a fever _____ noon.

K. They've been dating _____ five years.

L. I've been ready _____ three hours.

M. We've been studying _____ Friday.

N. I read _____ an hour.

WHEN?

These prepositions are used to talk about time: in, on, at, during, before, after, from, until, about.

We're going away in June.
Are you busy on Thursday?
Come over at 8:30.
Please don't talk during the movie.
We can buy our tickets an hour before the show starts.
That restaurant serves dinner from 5 until 11.
We'll stop by about 7.

FILL IN THE MISSING WORDS.
Choose the correct preposition.

A. The play begins _____at_____ 7:30. (at, on)

B. I work from 9 _____ 5. (after, until)

C. Come anytime _____ noon. (after, in)

D. I never wake up _____ 8 a.m. (before, on)

E. We're going out _____ the 14th. (at, on)

F. What are you doing _____ August? (at, in)

G. Let's go to Fern's Place _____ our lunch hour. (during, from)

H. I'm busy all week _____ Saturday. (in, until)

I. The movie plays _____ 1 until 3. (on, from)

J. Can you come over _____ 6? (about, in)

K. Let's get together _____ a week. (in, on)

L. I'll call her _____ her birthday. (at, on)

M. The party starts _____ 9:00. (at, on)

N. Are you usually busy _____ the evening? (during, on)

O. We'll see you again _____ the spring. (at, in)

P. Let's go out _____ work. (after, on)

Q. That store isn't open _____ noon. (before, in)

R. The flea market will be held _____ 2 until 5. (during, from)

S. You can only go to the post office _____ the day. (during, in)

T. The plane arrived _____ 4:47. (at, in)

U. The trains run _____ midnight. (in, until)

V. We have to make reservations _____ 6. (before, in)

W. Will you be free _____ a few days? (during, in)

X. Are you free _____ Thursday? (after, in)

Y. We'll be ready _____ fifteen minutes from now. (about, on)

Z. Where are you going _____ Monday? (at, on)

UNIT 5

LET ME BE HONEST WITH YOU

IN THIS UNIT, YOU WILL BE:

asking for someone's opinion about how to
    solve a personal problem
expressing fear, worry, or doubt about
    what is the right thing to do
offering an opinion
responding positively and negatively to an
    opinion
accepting that someone's opinion may be
    or is right
accepting criticism
asking for forgiveness or understanding
expressing approval or disapproval of
    someone's actions

In the Close-Up on Language, you will
review:

words that show how one thing, event, or
    idea is linked to another thing, event,
    or idea—prepositions of place,
    conjunctions, and verb tenses

LOOK AT THE PICTURE.
Find these things in the picture.

1. park bench
2. fence
3. gate
4. swings
5. slide

6. jungle gym/monkey bars
7. seesaw/teeter-totter
8. stroller
9. tricycle/trike
10. chess table

TALK TOPICS

LOOK AT THE PICTURE.
Talk about what you see.

What is this place?
Describe the people.   What are they
    doing?
Why do people come here?

Talk about the things in this playground.
    What do you do with these things?
    Is the swing safe for young children?
    Is the slide safe?

Why is one child running toward the
    gate?
Why is one child climbing out of his
    stroller?
Could these children get hurt?   How?
Do you think that their parents are
    careless?

Is this place only for children?
Would you come here alone?   What would
    you like to do here?
Is there a place like this in your
    neighborhood?   Where?

Pretend to be one of the people in the
    picture.   What were you doing on
    page 127?   What are you doing now?
    What are you saying?

ASK QUESTIONS ABOUT THE PICTURE.
Write down the new words and expressions you want to remember.

11. _____   16. _____
12. _____   17. _____
13. _____   18. _____
14. _____   19. _____
15. _____   20. _____

ASKING FOR AND GIVING OPINIONS

LISTEN TO THESE PEOPLE.
Two close friends are asking for and giving opinions.

DEBRA: Carmen, I need your opinion about something important. You know that I'm planning to go back to work. Should I hire a babysitter for the kids?

CARMEN: Well, I'm sure that a sitter would take good care of them. But if you ask me, a day care center might be better.

DEBRA: Why do you say that?

CARMEN: Well, I think that children should learn how to get along with other children. And I've heard that those centers have good programs.

DEBRA: Yes, but don't you think it's better for children to play at home? And don't you think that a babysitter would pay more attention to the kids?

CARMEN: The teachers in the center always keep an eye on the kids. And to be honest with you, I think children should be on their own a little bit. It makes them more responsible.

PETER: What's the matter, George? You look upset.

GEORGE: I just don't know what to do about my father. He's been so lonely and depressed since my mother died.

PETER: I know how it is. My aunt used to be like that. She's been happier since she moved into a senior citizens' building.

GEORGE: What's a senior citizens' building?

PETER: It's an apartment building for people who are 60 or older. I think that it's good for people to have friends their own age. They share a lot of the same problems and interests.

GEORGE: Don't you think it would be better if my father moved in with me?

PETER: I really don't know, George. I think that's for the two of you to decide.

GEORGE: Yes, you're right. Thanks.

PRACTICE USING THESE WORDS.
Find them in the conversations.
Write what they mean. Write new sentences with them.

A.   to pay attention _____

_____

B.   to keep an eye on (someone/something) _____

_____

C. to be on (their) own _____

_____

D. to know how it is _____

_____

E. to be good (or better) for (someone) _____

_____

TALK TOPICS
Look at the conversations on page 130.
Answer these questions in class.

A. What is a "day care center"? Do you know anyone with children in a day care center? What have they said about it? What is your opinion of day care centers?

B. What would you tell Debra? Do you agree with what Carmen said? Do you think that Debra should hire a babysitter? Why?

C. What is a "senior citizen"?

D. Is there a senior citizens' building in your community?

E. Some elderly people live in nursing homes. What is your opinion of nursing homes? Some elderly people live with their children. Do you think that's better?

F. What would you tell George? Do you agree with what Peter said? Do you think that George's father should live with George?

FILL IN THE MISSING WORDS.
Practice with another student.
Complete the conversations.

A parent is thinking about sending Tim, his/her 4-year-old child, to nursery school.
A friend is giving his/her opinion.

CONVERSATION A: The friend doesn't think Tim should go to nursery school.

PARENT: ____ you think that _____ ? (ask for friend's opinion)

FRIEND: ____ you ask ____ , I think you _____ keep Tim ____ home.

(give opinion)

PARENT: ____ you think that Tim _____ learn more ____ school? (express doubts)

FRIEND: To ____ honest ____ you, ____ think young children learn more ____ home.

(explain your opinion)

CONVERSATION B: The friend thinks Tim should go to nursery school.

PARENT: ____ you think that _____ ? (ask for friend's opinion)

FRIEND: ____ think that's ____ good idea. (give opinion)

PARENT: Don't _____ think that Tim _____ learn more ____ home?

(express doubts)

FRIEND: ____ be honest with ____ , I _____ young children learn more ____ school.

(explain your opinion)

TRY IT IN CLASS.
Practice with another student.

Use expressions like these:

PERSON ASKING FOR OPINION

I need your opinion about . . .
Do you think . . . ?
Don't you think . . . ?
How do you feel about . . .
What do you think about . . .
What would you do if . . .
Why do you say/think that . . . ?

PERSON GIVING OPINION

If you ask me . . .
I think . . .
To be honest with you . . .
I really don't know . . .
If I were you, I would . . .

A. A mother is planning to go back to work. Her parents said they would take care of her young son. Would that be good for her parents and her child? She is asking a friend.

Here are some reasons for and against leaving the child with his grandparents:

FOR

1. child should be with family
2. child will keep grandparents happy and busy
3. grandparents will watch child carefully

AGAINST

1. child should be with older children
2. child will make grandparents tired; grandparents need time to themselves
3. grandparents won't give child enough freedom and will spoil child

MOTHER

1. ask for opinion
2. express doubts (give a reason from the list)

FRIEND

1. give opinion—for or against
2. explain your opinion (give a reason from the list)

B. A person has been offered a better job in another city. He now lives near his parents. Should he move? He is asking a friend. (Note: Before you begin the conversation, list reasons for and against the move.)

THAT'S NOT TRUE!

LISTEN TO THESE PEOPLE.

Marta and her father are talking about
Marta's friend, Carla. Carla is going to
move into her own apartment.

Tom is disagreeing with his sister, Nancy.
They are talking about Tom's wife, Teresa,
who is planning to work outside the home.

MR. SANCHEZ: I can't believe Carla is
deserting her parents.

MARTA: Carla's not deserting her parents,
Father. She's only getting her own
apartment. I'm sure her parents will like
having time alone together.

MR. SANCHEZ: A girl should live with her
parents until she's married. She needs
someone to take care of her.

MARTA: Oh, come on, Father. She's old
enough to take care of herself. It'll be
good for her to be more independent.

MR. SANCHEZ: She should be saving her
money instead of paying rent. She'll
need money to set up house when she's
married.

MARTA: I'm sorry, but I think you're wrong.
She shouldn't plan her life around
getting married.

NANCY: Tom, I heard you're planning to put
my nephews in a day care center. Those
places are no good!

TOM: Now, that's not true, Nancy. We've
found an excellent place with a great
program and experienced teachers. It
will be good for the kids.

NANCY: I think it's terrible. Teresa has no
sense of responsibility towards her
children.

TOM: How can you say that? Teresa's not
irresponsible at all. Don't you see that
she's helping out the family by taking
this job?

NANCY: She belongs at home with her
children. That's all there is to it.

TOM: You don't understand, Nancy. Teresa
wants to go back to work, and we need
the money. We'll still spend a lot of time
with the children. They'll be fine. You'll
see.

PRACTICE USING THESE WORDS.
Find them in the conversations.
Write what they mean. Write new sentences with them.

A. not . . . at all _____

_____

B. don't you see _____

_____

133

C. to help out _____

_____

D. that's all there is to it _____

_____

E. to spend time _____

_____

F. you'll see _____

_____

TALK TOPICS
Look at the conversations on page 133.
Answer these questions in class.

A. What do you think of the way Marta talked to her father? Do you think she was disrespectful?

B. Why did Marta think that Carla should move? List the reasons. List other reasons why Carla should move.

    1. _____   **3.** _____

    2. _____   **4.** _____

C. Why did Mr. Sanchez think that Carla should live with her parents? List the reasons. List other reasons why Carla shouldn't move.

    1. _____   **3.** _____

    2. _____   **4.** _____

D. What do you think of the way that Nancy and Tom talked to each other?

E. Why did Tom think that his wife should work outside the home? List the reasons. List other reasons why Teresa should work outside the home.

    1. _____   **3.** _____

    2. _____   **4.** _____

F. Why did Nancy think that Teresa shouldn't work outside the home? List the reasons. List other reasons why Teresa shouldn't work outside the home.

    1. _____   **3.** _____

    2. _____   **4.** _____

TRY IT IN CLASS.
Practice with another student.
One student states an opinion. The other student disagrees with that opinion.

Use expressions like these:

STATING AN OPINION	DISAGREEING WITH AN OPINION
I believe . . .	That's not true.
I know . . .	That's just not so.
I feel . . .	How can you say that?
	Don't you see that . . .
	You don't understand . . .
	I'm sorry, but . . .

A. Two parents are talking about their 20-year-old daughter. Their daughter wants to get her own apartment.
(Look at page 134, B and C. Use the lists in your conversation.)

MOTHER	FATHER
1. you don't want daughter to move—give a reason	1. you accept daughter's decision—give a reason
2. disagree; give a reason	2. disagree; give a reason
3. disagree; give a reason	3. disagree; give a reason

B. A brother and sister are talking about their sister. Their sister is planning to work outside the home. She is married and has a 7-year-old child.
(Look at page 134, E and F. Use the lists in your conversation.)

SISTER	BROTHER
1. you're glad your sister is going back to work—give a reason	1. you think your sister should stay at home—give a reason
2. disagree; give a reason	2. disagree; give a reason
3. disagree; give a reason	3. disagree; give a reason

C. Two parents are talking about their son. He wants to take care of his children while his wife works. He does not plan to work outside the home.

MOTHER	FATHER
1. you're glad son is going to stay at home with children	1. you think son should work— daughter-in-law should stay at home
2. disagree; give a reason	2. disagree; give a reason

YOU MAY BE RIGHT

LISTEN TO THESE PEOPLE.
Frank and Lee are close friends.   Frank is responding to Lee's opinion.

FRANK: I've been offered that job in the city, Lee.   I think I'm going to take it.

LEE: You don't seem too excited about it.

FRANK: Well, I'm not.   I really like my job. And I'm not looking forward to driving an hour to work.   But I have to take it.   It's more money.

LEE: Now, Frank, you don't have to do anything.   Think of all the time you spend at work.   Why take a job you don't like?

FRANK: You've got a point, Lee.   But I have to think about my family.   We need the money.

LEE: Your family needs you too, Frank.   With that long drive to work, they'll never see you.

FRANK: You may be right.   Still, I hate to pass up that salary.

LEE: Why don't you talk to your boss about a raise?   And keep looking for another job.   Don't just take the first one that comes along.

FRANK: You're right.   Thanks for the advice.

PRACTICE USING THESE WORDS.
Find them in the conversation.
Write what they mean.   Write new sentences with them.

A.   to look forward to (something) _____

_____

B.   to have a point _____

_____

C.   to pass (something) up _____

_____

D.   to come along _____

_____

136

TALK TOPICS
Look at the conversation on page 136.
Answer these questions in class.

A. Do you agree with Lee? Do you think that Lee should have given Frank his opinion?

B. In the beginning of their conversation, did Frank agree with Lee? At the end of their conversation, did Frank agree with Lee?

FILL IN THE MISSING WORDS.
Practice with another student.
Complete the conversations.

Maria's company has offered to send her to computer training school.
Maria isn't sure she should go.
Maria's husband, Dan, is trying to persuade her to go.

DAN: _____ don't you want _____ go to school, Maria? (ask for reason)

MARIA: _____ think it will _____ too hard. (give reason)

DAN: Believe me, _____ can do it. _____ sure you can. (persuade)

MARIA: _____ guess so. But _____ will I have time _____ do the homework?

(express doubts)

DAN: You _____ do it _____ weekends. You've always wanted _____ go.

Now' _____ your chance. (persuade)

MARIA: You've _____ a point. But what _____ I don't like it? (express doubts)

DAN: You _____ give it a try. It's only for _____ couple _____ weeks. (persuade)

MARIA: That' _____ true. _____ right. (agree completely)

Kim has been asked to join a bowling team.
Kim isn't sure she should join.
Kim's friend, Yoko, is trying to persuade her to join.

YOKO: _____ don't you want _____ join the team, Kim? (ask for reason)

KIM: _____ don't think I'_____ good enough. (give reason)

YOKO: Yes _____ are. That' _____ why they asked you to join. (persuade)

KIM: _____ guess so, but _____ will I have time _____ practice? (express doubts)

YOKO: You _____ practice after work. (persuade)

KIM: _____ right. I'll join. (agree)

Practice with another student.
One friend is trying to persuade another.

The friend who is being persuaded should use expressions like these:

You may/might be right.
Maybe you're right.
You've got a point.
I guess so, but . . .

You're right.
That's true.
That's right.
I agree with you.

A. Two friends who live in different towns are on the telephone. One friend is trying to persuade the other friend to visit him/her.

FRIEND A	FRIEND B
1. invite friend to visit you	1. you can't, but thank friend for asking
2. ask for reason why friend can't come	2. you're too busy at work
3. say that friend is always busy at work—he/she needs time off	3. agree, but you have no transportation to friend's house
4. say that friend can take train; you'll pick friend up at train station	4. agree, but you don't have money for hotel room
5. say that friend can stay with you	5. agree to come

B. Two friends who work in the same company are talking. One friend has seen another employee take money from the petty cash box. He/she isn't sure whether or not to tell the boss. The other friend is trying to persuade him/her to tell the boss.

FRIEND A	FRIEND B
1. ask if friend is going to tell boss about theft	1. you don't think so
2. ask for reason	2. you don't want to get involved
3. say that friend is involved— he/she saw theft	3. agree; but you don't want to betray other employee
4. say that other employee was wrong; friend shouldn't help him/her	4. agree to tell boss

C. Two friends who share an apartment are talking. The utilities company made a mistake on their utilities bill. The company didn't charge them enough. One friend is trying to persuade the other friend to tell the utilities company.

I'M REALLY SORRY

LISTEN TO THESE PEOPLE.
They are accepting criticism.

MARIA: José, we just got a late payment notice from the hardware store. I thought we paid that bill.

JOSÉ: Oh, I forgot all about it. I'm sorry.

MARIA: How could you be so careless? Now we'll have to pay a late charge.

JOSÉ: You're right, I was careless. I've just been so busy lately. It completely slipped my mind. Try to understand.

MARIA: I'm sorry that I was tough on you. I know that you've been under pressure. It was inconsiderate of me to get mad at you.

JOSÉ: That's OK. I understand why you were angry. I'll take care of the bill right away.

MARIA: Don't worry about it. I'll do it.

MIKE: Why did you make plans for Saturday night without asking me?

BETTY: I'm really sorry, Mike. I didn't think you'd mind.

MIKE: I wanted to get some rest this weekend. Now I'm going to have to spend the evening with Gary and Ellen.

BETTY: It was inconsiderate of me. I should have asked you. But I thought you liked Gary and Ellen.

MIKE: No, I don't. Gary's too irritable and Ellen's too serious. They're not much fun.

BETTY: How can you say that? They're my best friends!

MIKE: I'm sorry. That was thoughtless.

BETTY: Well, from now on I'll ask you before I make plans for us. And I hope you'll try harder to like my friends.

PRACTICE USING THESE WORDS.
Find them in the conversations.
Write what they mean. Write new sentences with them.

A. it slipped my mind _____

_____

B. to be tough on (someone) _____

_____

C. to be under pressure _____

_____

D. to take care of (something) _____

_____

E. from now on _____

_____

TALK TOPICS
Look at the conversations on page 139.
Answer these questions in class.

A. Do you think that José was "careless"? Do you think that Maria was "inconsiderate"?

B. Both Maria and José apologized to each other. Would you apologize if you were Maria? Would you apologize if you were José?

C. Do you think that Betty was "inconsiderate"? Do you think that Mike was "thoughtless"?

D. Both Mike and Betty apologized to each other. Would you apologize if you were Mike? Would you apologize if you were Betty?

TALK TO THESE PEOPLE.
What would you say in each situation? How would you apologize?

A. You were supposed to meet a friend at a restaurant. You forgot. Your friend calls you.

FRIEND: Where were you? We were supposed to meet an hour ago.

YOU: _____

B. Your husband/wife's parents gave you a gift. You never thanked them for it.

HUSBAND/WIFE: Why didn't you thank them? That was thoughtless.

YOU: _____

C. You borrowed a sweater from a friend. You got a stain on it.

FRIEND: May I have my sweater?

YOU: _____

D. You were invited to a party. You didn't want to go. You never answered the invitation.

SISTER/BROTHER: Why didn't you tell them you weren't coming? That was really rude.

YOU: _____

TRY IT IN CLASS.
Practice with another student.
One person is criticizing another.
The other person accepts the criticism.

The person who is accepting the criticism should use expressions like these:

I'm sorry.
I apologize.
You're right.
I understand why . . .
From now on . . .
Next time, I'll . . .
I didn't think . . .
I should have . . .

A. A parent is criticizing his/her teenage son for coming home late.

PARENT	**SON**
1. tell son that you're upset—he was late and you were worried	1. apologize—you didn't think parents would worry
2. say that son should have called to say he would be late	2. agree; admit you were thoughtless
3. tell son to call you the next time	3. agree; apologize again

B. A parent is criticizing his/her teenage daughter. The daughter took the family car without permission.

PARENT	**DAUGHTER**
1. tell daughter that you're upset—she took the car and you needed it	1. apologize—you didn't think anyone needed the car
2. say that daughter should have asked permission	2. agree; admit you were inconsiderate
3. tell daughter to ask you the next time	3. agree; apologize again

C. A wife is criticizing her husband. The husband made plans without asking his wife.

WIFE	**HUSBAND**
1. tell husband that you're upset—you don't want to go out tonight	1. apologize—you thought she would like to go out
2. say that husband should have asked you before he made plans	2. agree; admit you made a mistake
3. tell husband to ask you the next time	3. agree; apologize again

EXPRESSING APPROVAL AND DISAPPROVAL

LISTEN TO THESE PEOPLE.
One person is asking for an opinion. The other person is expressing approval or disapproval.

SUE: There is a job opening at HealthCare Pharmacy, Father. I'd like to apply for it. What do you think?

MR. LUCK: Do you have time for a job? You're so busy with your schoolwork. I don't think I approve of the idea.

SUE: It's only three nights a week. I'd be finished work at 9:00.

MR. LUCK: That might be OK. Do you honestly think you'll have time for your homework?

SUE: Yes, I do.

MR. LUCK: That's my only worry. I'm all for it, then.

BILL: What do you think of my new apartment, Mother?

MRS. NEWMAN: Well, I like it better than your old apartment. It was smart of you to leave that place.

BILL: Yes, I know you didn't care for my last apartment. But how do you like this one?

MRS. NEWMAN: It's not a bad place. The rent isn't too high, either.

BILL: Do you mean that you approve of my living here?

MRS. NEWMAN: I still don't think you should live alone. But if you have to, I guess I approve of this apartment.

Angela is disapproving of a friend's behavior. George is approving of a friend's behavior.

ANGELA: I think Carmen is too tough on those kids. Sometimes she's really mean to them.

GEORGE: No she's not, Angela. Carmen is a good mother. You just have to be very firm with children.

ANGELA: Well, I don't think it's good to yell at them all the time. Kids need to be treated with respect too.

GEORGE: You're just too easy on them, Angela. Carmen is doing a good job with those kids.

PRACTICE USING THESE WORDS.
Find them in the conversations.
Write what they mean. Write new sentences with them.

A. to be all for (something) _____

_____

B. to care for (something) _____

_____

C. to be mean to (someone) _____

_____

D. to be firm with (someone) _____

_____

E. to be easy on (someone) _____

_____

TALK TOPICS
Look at the conversations on page 142.
Answer these questions in class.

A. In the beginning of their conversation, did Mr. Luck approve of
Sue's idea? Why?
At the end of their conversation, did Mr. Luck approve of Sue's
idea? Why?

B. Did Mrs. Newman think that Bill should live alone?
Did Mrs. Newman approve of Bill's apartment?

C. Did Angela approve of Carmen's behavior? Why?
Did George approve of Carmen's behavior? Why?

D. Read these situations. Would you approve or disapprove?
  1. Your friend wants to buy a motorcycle. She needs it to ride to
     work.
  2. Your son wants to join a football team.
  3. Your friend wants to quit his job. He plans to spend a year
     travelling and working at part-time jobs.

Use expressions like these:

EXPRESSING APPROVAL	**EXPRESSING DISAPPROVAL**
I approve of . . .	I don't approve of . . .
I'm all for it.	I disapprove.

A. Two friends are talking about their friend, Carmen. Carmen is planning to move back to her native country. One friend approves of the idea. Another friend disapproves of the idea.

FRIEND A	**FRIEND B**
1. Carmen is moving back to native country; you approve of her plans	1. say that you disapprove of her plans
2. you think Carmen did try, but she misses her family	2. you think it will be hard to go back
3. you think it's harder to stay here	3. disagree, but you hope Carmen will be happier

B. A mother and father are talking about their teenage son. He wants to quit school and get a job. The mother disapproves of her son's decision. The father approves.

MOTHER	**FATHER**
1. say that you disapprove of son's decision—he should stay in school	1. say that you approve of son's decision—he should get a job
2. you think son is making a mistake—education is important	2. you think son can learn more by working
3. you don't think son can get a good job	3. you think son will get a good job

C. Two friends are talking about their friend, Marta. Marta is planning to get married. The man she is going to marry is 10 years younger than she is. One friend disapproves of the marriage. The other friend approves.

FRIEND A	**FRIEND B**
1. say that you disapprove of Marta's marriage plans	1. say that you approve of Marta's marriage plans
2. you think she should marry someone her own age	2. you disagree; age doesn't matter
3. you don't think Marta and her husband will have the same interests	3. you think they'll be happy together

TRY IT IN CLASS.
Many radio stations across the United States have "talk shows."
People call the talk show host to discuss their opinions and ask for advice.

Have a talk show in class. One student is the host. The host leads the discussion. The other students are the callers.

Choose from these possible calls:

A. I think Americans are terrible to the elderly. Americans don't respect people over 65. Older people are no longer treated as part of society. Do you agree that Americans act this way? Are the elderly treated this way in other countries?

B. Children have rights too. They should help make decisions in the family. Too many people just tell their children what to do. Do you agree?

C. I think movie ratings are stupid. Only parents should decide what their children should see. What do you think?

D. I think alcohol should be illegal. It's the cause of many traffic accidents, family problems, and problems at work. What do you think?

E. My son wants to change his name to "Ernie." He says that his name—"Enrique"—doesn't sound American. I think he should be proud of the name we gave him. He says he is only trying to fit into American society. What do you think?

F. My father has lived by himself since my mother died. Now he is sick and needs someone to take care of him. Both my wife and I work during the day. What should we do?

G. My daughter lives with my wife and me. She's 25 years old. She has a good job. Do you think she should give us a little money for rent and food?

H. I don't like what they teach kids in school. There's too much career training. I think they should teach them more about history, art, and music. What do you think?

I. Americans spend too much time watching TV. I think watching TV is a waste of time. Do you agree?

J. My 16-year-old granddaughter goes out on dates. I think she's too young to date. Her parents say that she's old enough. Do you agree with them or with me?

K. Married women shouldn't be allowed to work. They belong in the home. Working women are bad for the family. And there aren't enough jobs for both men and women. Do you agree?

CLOSE-UP ON LANGUAGE

PREPOSITIONS

Notice how the following prepositions show the relationship between a person or thing and a place.

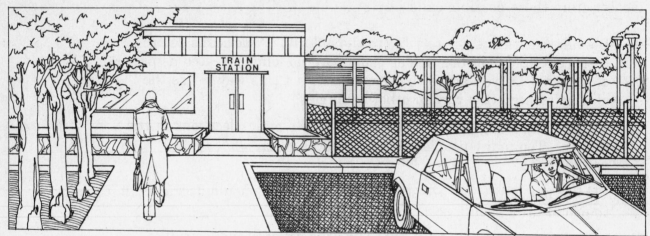

He walked _to_ the train station.   She drove home _from_ the train station.

He stood _at_ the bus stop.
He stood _on_ the sidewalk.

The gas station was _off_ the main road.
The car was _in_ the garage.

FILL IN THE MISSING WORDS.
Choose the correct preposition.

A.   They went _____to_____ the gym.   (at, to)

B.   The plates are _____ the table.   (in, on)

C.   He ran _____ the door.   (off, to)

D.   I walked _____ the bank to his house.   (at, from)

E.   Keep the dog _____ the furniture.   (in, off)

F. They stayed _____ the hotel.   (at, from)

G. She met me _____ Los Angeles.   (in, on)

H. I'll see you _____ Yung's house.   (at, on)

I. He sat _____ the sofa.   (at, on)

J. The picture fell _____ the wall.   (off, on)

K. I put the milk _____ the refrigerator.   (in, to)

L. She moved here _____ her native country, Korea.   (from, off)

M. We're going _____ the restaurant.   (at, to)

N. I spoke to him _____ the office.   (at, off)

O. That town is _____ the main road.   (at, off)

P. Stay away _____ my house.   (from, to)

Q. My coat was _____ the living room.   (at, in)

R. Your shoes are _____ the floor.   (at, on)

Notice how the following prepositions show the position of things in relation to each other.

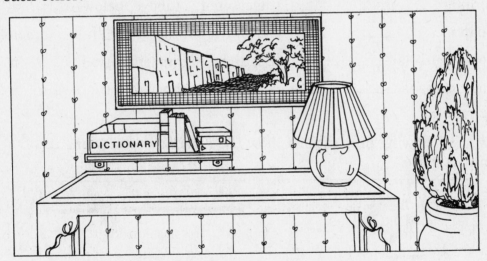

The picture is above the table.
The table is below the picture.
The shelf is over the table.
The table is under the shelf.
The plant is by the table.   The plant is beside the table.
The lamp is on top of the table.
The table is in front of the wall.
The wall is in back of the table.   The wall is behind the table.
The shelf is between the picture and the table.
The dictionary is among the books.

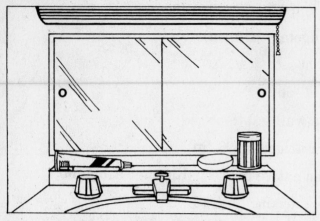

FILL IN THE MISSING WORDS.
Look at the picture. Choose the correct preposition.

A. The soap is _____ by _____ the glass.   (behind, by)

B. The cabinet is _____ the sink.   (above, below)

C. The toothpaste is _____ the sink.   (in front of, on top of)

D. The cabinet is _____ the light and the sink.   (among, between)

E. The light is _____ the cabinet.   (over, under)

F. The sink is _____ the cabinet.   (above, below)

G. The soap is _____ the things on top of the sink.   (among, between)

H. The toothbrush is _____ the toothpaste.   (in back of, in front of)

I. The toothpaste is _____ the toothbrush.   (in back of, in front of)

Notice how the following prepositions show the direction or movement
of a person in a place.

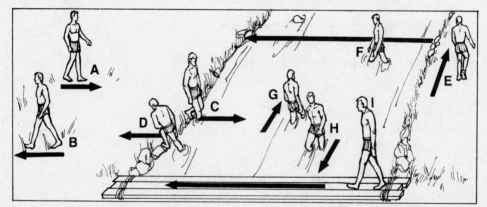

A. He is walking <u>toward</u> the stream.

B. He is walking <u>away from</u> the stream.

C. He walked <u>into</u> the stream.

D. He walked <u>out of</u> the stream.

E. He is walking <u>along</u> the stream.

F. He is walking <u>through</u> the stream.

G. He is walking <u>up</u> the stream.

H. He is walking <u>down</u> the stream.

I. He is walking <u>across</u> the stream.

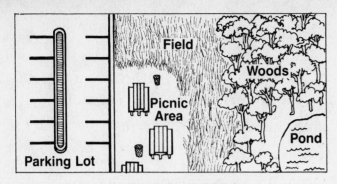

FILL IN THE MISSING WORDS.
Look at the picture. Choose the correct preposition.

You are in the parking lot.

A. To get to the woods, walk _____through_____ the field.   (through, up)

B. To get to the pond, walk _____ the field.   (across, along)

C. To get to the field, walk _____ the woods.   (toward, out of)

You are in the field.

A. To get to the parking lot, walk _____ the woods.   (away from, toward)

B. To get to the pond, walk _____ the woods.   (along, into)

C. To get to the woods, walk _____ the field.   (into, out of)

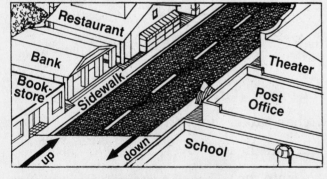

FILL IN THE MISSING WORDS.
Review the prepositions you have learned.
Look at the picture. Choose the correct preposition.

You are standing on the sidewalk outside the bank.

A. To get to the restaurant, walk _____up_____ the street.   (across, up)

B. To get to the bookstore, walk _____ the street.   (down, up)

C. To get to the post office, walk _____ the street.   (across, up)

You are standing on the sidewalk outside the post office.

A. To get to the school, walk _____ the street.   (across, down)

B. To get to the theater, walk _____ the street.   (down, up)

C. To get to the bank, walk _____ the street.   (across, up)

FILL IN THE MISSING WORDS.
Choose the correct preposition.

A. Please put the pot _____on_____ the stove.   (on, up)

B. There is a bus stop _____ the grocery store.   (in front of, to)

C. Can you go _____ the bank this afternoon?   (at, to)

D. My gloves are _____ my pocket.   (between, in)

E. She put the letter _____ the two books.   (between, in)

F. Put your shoes _____ the bed.   (through, under)

G. May I hang my coat _____ his?   (between, on top of)

H. They are running _____ us.   (away from, through)

I. Who's that man walking _____ the house?   (at, toward)

J. Would you like to walk _____ the park?   (on, through)

K. They're showing a movie _____ the library.   (at, on)

L. I was walking _____ the door when you called.   (across, out)

M. There's a sharp pain _____ my knee.   (at, below)

N. They jogged _____ the hill.   (in, up)

O. The picture is _____ the sofa.   (above, among)

P. The library is _____ the street.   (across, through)

Q. They swam _____ the river.   (down, out)

R. We came here _____ the movies.   (at, from)

S. Get the cat _____ the kitchen table.   (off, on)

T. There's a bird flying _____ your head.   (over, under)

U. We ran _____ the house.   (into, up)

V. The table is _____ the bed.   (beside, through)

W. Your letter is _____ the letters on my desk.   (among, between)

X. There's a mouse _____ the refrigerator.   (across, behind)

Y. My shoes are _____ the closet.   (in, on)

Z. The dresser is _____ the mirror.   (at, below)

CONJUNCTIONS

Conjunctions show a relationship between ideas.
Review these conjunctions: <u>and</u>, <u>or</u>, <u>but</u>, <u>so</u>, <u>because</u>.

Tom went to the bank. Rita went to the post office.
Tom went to the bank, <u>and</u> Rita went to the post office.

We can eat at a restaurant. We can eat at home.
We can eat at a restaurant, <u>or</u> we can eat at home.

Don went to the movies. His sister stayed home.
Don went to the movies, <u>but</u> his sister stayed home.

The movie was terrible. I left before it was over.
The movie was terrible, <u>so</u> I left before it was over.

Bring a raincoat. It's going to rain.
Bring a raincoat <u>because</u> it's going to rain.

WRITE SENTENCES.
Use a conjunction.

A. You can smoke in the lobby. You can't smoke in the theater.

  You can smoke in the lobby, but you can't smoke in the theater.

B. Please fill out the application. Then fill out the deposit slip.

_____

C. Would you like tea? Would you rather have coffee?

_____

D. The train didn't come. I walked to work.

_____

E. Our radio is broken. We can't afford another one.

_____

F. Take a look at the car. Make me an offer.

_____

G. We didn't have any food. I went to the grocery store.

_____

H. We can drive home. We can walk home.

_____

I. The napkins are in the kitchen. The plates are in the dining room.

_____

The following conjunctions show a time relationship between two actions.

I'll call you <u>when</u> I get home.
Please fill out this form <u>while</u> you're waiting.
We've known each other <u>since</u> we were children.
Put on a coat <u>before</u> you go outside.
Let's take a walk <u>after</u> the rain stops.
You can't go to lunch <u>until</u> the store is clean.

FILL IN THE MISSING WORDS.
Choose the correct conjunction.

A. I'll start saving money _____ I get a raise.   (when, since)

B. I'll buy a coat _____ I get paid.   (after, until)

C. I'll make the deposit for you _____ you fill out the forms.   (until, while)

D. Come back _____ lunch is over.   (after, while)

E. Please don't smoke _____ you're in line.   (before, while)

F. Put this letter in the mailbox _____ the mail carrier comes.   (before, while)

G. You can wait on the customers _____ lunch.   (after, while)

H. You should shop around _____ you buy a car.   (before, since)

I. He's been happier _____ he moved to the apartment.   (since, while)

J. Don't go outside _____ you feel better.   (after, until)

K. I won't be able to get a car _____ I learn how to drive.   (since, until)

L. I haven't been hungry _____ I went on a diet.   (before, since)

M. Make sure to have money _____ you go shopping.   (until, when)

N. Mothers should stay home _____ their kids are young.   (before, while)

O. She played the guitar _____ he sang.   (since, while)

P. I've been working _____ I was 16.   (before, since)

Q. Call me _____ you're not busy.   (after, when)

R. Let's go to a restaurant _____ we see the movie.   (after, while)

S. We went shopping _____ we made dinner.   (before, while)

T. The baby cries _____ he is hungry.   (after, when)

U. Have a seat _____ you're waiting for the doctor.   (before, while)

V. I've been taking care of her _____ she's been sick.   (since, until)

W. Let's clean the house _____ the guests arrive.   (before, while)

X. Don't talk to him _____ you calm down.   (since, until)

152

VERB TENSES

Verb tenses signal how actions are related in time.

Notice how the tenses in this sentence signal which action comes first:

When Rick <u>comes</u> home, we <u>will call</u> you. (present tense + future tense)

Notice how the tenses in this sentence signal which action is happening now and which action is completed.

I <u>know</u> that you <u>were</u> busy yesterday. (present tense + past tense)

Notice how the tenses in this sentence signal which past action happened first:

Rita <u>had gone</u> out before we <u>arrived</u>. (past perfect tense + past tense)

REWRITE THE SENTENCES.
Each sentence contains more than one verb.
Change only the underlined verb.
Show an appropriate time relationship.

A. I <u>knew</u> we will finish the job.

I know we will finish the job.

B. He realized that he <u>met</u> her before.

C. I think that I <u>lose</u> my scarf.

D. He had already eaten dinner when we <u>come</u>.

E. I'm glad that you <u>take</u> the job.

F. He <u>believed</u> that she'll visit him.

G. She had been sick for two days before she <u>call</u> the doctor.

H. I <u>thought</u> that you'll win.

I. He <u>likes</u> the present you give him.